AF571903

JESUS: the whole in one

H.B.* & His/Her Bible Adventures

Volume 7

by H.B. George Harper

* Human Being

Library of Congress Catalog Card Number: 86-82884
ISBN 0-937959-12-X

Published by H.B. Publications,
38 Cloverview, Helena, Montana 59601

Publishing Consultant:
Falcon Press Publishing Co., Inc.,
Helena and Billings, Montana

CONTENTS

DOWN . . .

Down on the shore of the lake the fishermen worked to mend their nets, worked at the familiar way of life.

Down where the safety of the oft-trod shore and the dangerous adventure of the trackless deep are constantly pulling a man in two directions.

Down where the beauty of dawn and sunset and the awe-filling havoc of the blasting storm take their turn in teaching a man to be both sensitive and strong.

Down where a man always wonders what the next day will be like, where a man's own plans always are subject to revision by a nature of things beyond his control.

Down where the waves reflected the restlessness of their own souls.

Down there they saw Him coming toward them for the first time.

And suddenly the lake was calm with the hushed waiting of something mighty to come. Their busy fingers left off their mending. Under all the big sky, beside the vast lake there was only this Man who walked toward them.

The force of His personality reached to them even before He spoke a word.

They sensed that once again they must make the choice between the safety of the shallows and the adventure of the deep. This time forever.

"COME, FOLLOW ME!"

UP. . .

Up from their nets they rose.

Up from the perpetual indecision of life at the edge.

Up toward a destiny which they would seek in His company, these sons of men rose to follow this Son of Man.

And before many more storms had beat themselves out on the rugged lake shore they would come to know this Son of Man as the Son of God.

Down by the lakeside that day they determined to follow Jesus, the man.

Up on the mountaintops of their own experience in days to come, they would learn to recognize Jesus, the Christ, as God's own self-revelation.

Up from the edge of life to its center, from the shallows to the deep, they made their start that day. And they walked with Him until they found themselves, like the dawn and sunset, the storm and the calm, to be a fitting part of God's Great Plan.

Shall we go with them on this journey into life following this Jesus who called to them and calls also to us?

This re-reading of the Gospel story can be our attempt to catch up with them after a twenty century head start.

Even now, through their eyes and ears, we can walk with Jesus the Man also. And through their minds and hearts we can sense again the wonder of how God can be so especially incarnate in Jesus the Christ.

Here on the modern edge of our own life, our own restless souls stir to hear this Man interpret the meaning of it all in the plain language of this world. Right down here on our shoreline we want to see a real flesh and blood Man live His human life in this real world. And in the living of it reveal to us the God who made it and us.

Jesus: The whole in one.
"COME, FOLLOW ME!"

Introduction

When the armed mob took Jesus in the Garden of Gethsemane they grabbed a youthful follower of Jesus who had tagged along after the group when they left the city that evening. But he wriggled right out of his clothes and ran away stark naked into the night.

When James, the apostle, was killed by King Herod and Peter was put into prison (*Acts*, chapter 12), some of the Christians of Jerusalem had a prayer meeting in the house of the mother of that young man. It must have been a regular meeting place, because when Peter made his escape from jail he hurried right to John Mark's house.

Paul and Barnabas were in Jerusalem, having come with contributions from the church in Antioch to the Jerusalem Christians since persecution and famine conditions had hit them hard. When they returned to Antioch, and then went from there to Paul's first mission journey, they took young John Mark with them as a helper.

In later years the early church writer, Papias (about 140 A.D.) refers to Mark as the "interpreter of Peter."

So from personal experience as a youth with Jesus, and from listening often to Peter's accounts of Jesus' days of ministry on earth, Mark was in a good position to be the first person to write a "Gospel." Both

Matthew and Luke later used Mark's writing as the main source of their information.

In 64 or 65 A.D., thirty years or so after Jesus, the time came for him to put his story into final writing. Mark was in Rome, and Rome was a city full of bitterness. One old story says that the great fire that swept Rome that winter was blamed on the Christians, and that Emperor Nero was using them as scapegoats for the disaster.

Now, as the fury of persecution broke upon them and the Roman Christians had to decide whether this new cause actually was worth dying for, Mark gave them the story of the Christ who was victorious over persecution and death.

To read this simple, forceful story of how Jesus the man demonstrated Himself to be the Christ, the Son of God, gave those persecuted Christians a courage that comes when a person knows that she or he is on the right side. They could depend on their Christ to continue to be victorious.

A few years later, the writers of both *Matthew* and *Luke* added to Mark's briefer book stories and accounts they had found from other sources. That's what we are going to do as we make one Gospel account out of the three synoptic Gospels of *Matthew*, *Mark* and *Luke*. We will follow the basic story in *Mark* and add in *Matthew* and *Luke* everywhere they stuck in their own additions. Here is the whole story of Jesus as they tell it the way it was told to them.

John takes such a different approach to the Jesus story and message that we will read his contribution separately. Otherwise, we would get hopelessly entangled in who said what when and where.

MATTHEW, MARK, LUKE

The Whole Jesus Story

The great Hebrew prophet, Isaiah, predicted once that God would someday send the Messiah (Christ is the Greek word) into the world. In order to prepare for His coming, God would send another man ahead of Him to preach that people should get ready to receive the Christ.

"Behold, I will send a messenger who will prepare the way; He will be a voice calling out in the wilderness, 'Get ready for God's coming; straighten up your lives.'"

That man was John the Baptist. At the time Jesus was a young man in Nazareth, John was preaching in the desert near the Jordan River. He not only preached; he challenged people to be baptized as a sign that they really wanted to live as God expected them to live. Lots of people from around Jerusalem went out to hear John preach, and many of them publicly confessed their sins and were baptized.

John was a rough desert man in appearance. He ate locusts and wild honey and dressed in a camel hair cloak with a leather belt around his waist. There was one thing he kept saying:

"Someone else is coming after me who is a much better representative of God than I am. In fact, I am not good enough to hold His coat for Him. I have baptized you with water, but He will baptize you with the Holy Spirit.'' (*Mark* 1:1-8)

Who was this John who is pictured in all the Gospels as the forerunner for Jesus? Luke picked up a story or two about John's family, and he did what he says in the short introduction to his accounts of the time of Jesus and the beginnings of the Christian movement. Some of those accounts are from eyewitnesses; others have been passed on by word of mouth. And for some time Luke had been trying to collect them all, edit them, and put them in order so that some important person named Theophilus, and we, could read them. (*Luke* 1:1-4) This is what Luke had learned about John:

''When Herod was king in Judea, a priest named Zechariah had married a woman, also from the family of Aaron. Her name was Elizabeth. Both of them were good people who tried to keep all the rules of their religion so that they would be blameless in God's sight. Though they were getting old, they had no children.

''One day when Zechariah was on duty in the temple, he was the person chosen by casting lots to represent the other priests as the one to enter the inner temple and burn incense. Everybody else stayed outside and prayed while he performed that duty inside. An angel appeared on the right side of the altar of incense. Zechariah was understandably surprised and nervous, but the angel quickly put him at ease by saying 'There is nothing to be afraid of. I come with good news, in fact. Your prayers for a child have been heard, and Elizabeth is going to have a son. Call his name John. Not only will you two be happy, but many people will be glad because John will be a great servant of God. He will fulfill the 'Nazarite' vow (*Numbers* 6:3) not ever to take strong drink. From birth he will be filled with the Holy Spirit, and he will cause many people of Israel to repent. He will be a forerunner like Elijah, making people ready for the Lord to come into their lives.'

"How can this be?" Zechariah stammered out. "My wife and I are too old to have a child!"

"I am Gabriel (one of the seven archangels Jewish traditions named in those days). I came here from the presence of God to tell you. It's going to happen, all right, but because you doubted me, you will not be able to speak a word until the child is born!"

The people knew something was delaying Zechariah's return to them, and when he came out they could see from his face that he had seen a vision inside. He tried to tell them, but couldn't make a sound. Seeing him make signs with his hands as he pointed at his throat and mouth, they realized that he had lost his voice. For the rest of his week on duty, he worked without speaking, then hurried home to be with Elizabeth.

Just as the angel had predicted, Elizabeth got pregnant and for five months she stayed in seclusion, hardly able to believe that the child she had wanted all her adult life was finally coming even though she had thought she was much too old ever to conceive a child.

"Elizabeth was six months into her pregnancy when the angel Gabriel made another trip. This time he went to Nazareth, a little city in Galilee about 70 miles north of Jerusalem, to speak to a young girl named Mary. The average Jewish girl was married by 13 years of age to a young man of 18. Probably a young teenager, though already living with a man named Joseph in the first stage of marriage, Mary had no idea what the angel meant when he said, 'Greetings, favored one, the Lord is with you! Don't be afraid, (that's the first thing an angel says to anybody in the *Bible* stories: don't be afraid) God thinks you are worthy to have a special son. Call Him Jesus.'"

Then, just as he had in the announcement to Elizabeth, Gabriel breaks into poetry:

"He will be great, and will be called the Son of God;
The Lord will put Him on the throne of David,
And He will reign forever over Israel in a never-ending kingdom!"

"How can this be?" Mary asked in amazement. "We have not yet culminated our marriage."

"Your pregnancy will be an act of the Holy Spirit, so the child in you will be the Son of God in a special way," Gabriel assured her. "And I'll tell you something else, perhaps even more amazing, your kinswoman Elizabeth is also pregnant, as old as she is! She is already six months along, and everybody said she could never have a child. You see, nothing is impossible with God."

"Well, I am God's servant. I accept whatever comes." And with that word from Mary the angel departed.

There was one sure way to check out the story and to share it with the one other person who would understand when she said she had talked with an angel. As soon as she could arrange to get away, Mary headed out for a visit with Elizabeth. All the way as she walked cross-country to the hills of Judah outside Jerusalem, she wondered how she would be received. She need not have worried. As soon as she went into the house, the baby in Elizabeth seemed to kick with joy, and the older woman felt compelled by the Spirit of God to practically shout: "Mary, you are blessed among women, and your baby will be specially blessed! I knew when you spoke, and my baby jumped inside me, that you were the one would would be the mother of my Lord. You believed the angel and are ready to play your part in this divine drama which is unfolding!"

Like Hannah in *I Samuel* 2:1-10, Mary is inspired,

Luke says (1:47-55), and says or sings the poetry that fit the high moment she and Elizabeth shared. Some old manuscripts attributed the song to Elizabeth as she continued speaking to Mary. Millions of Christians know this passage today as the "Magnificat" from the first words in Latin:

"My soul magnifies the Lord, and my spirit rejoices in God my Savior."

(If you want something to be seen more plainly, you magnify it. What a wonderfully incredible thing for a young person to say: *My* soul magnifies the Lord!)

"I am just a common person, not famous and not wealthy, but from now on I will be remembered as important. This is God's doing entirely, and in every generation God shows great compassion for those who are faithful. The proud people who think in their hearts that they are so special get put down, even the mighty rulers on thrones, and people who are lowly are raised up by God. The humble people have their hungers filled, while those who trust in their own riches are sent away empty. This is what God is doing again for little Israel as our ancestors were promised!"

For three months, until the time came for Elizabeth to have her baby, Mary stayed to help Elizabeth. When that great day came, all the neighbors and kinsfolk were on hand to congratulate her, almost as excited as she and Zechariah were. They were sure that the child would be given the father's name, Zechariah, when the boy was circumcised on the eighth day.

"Zechariah will be a wonderful name for the baby," they agreed.

"No, we are going to call him 'John,'" Elizabeth told them.

"What? There isn't a man anywhere in your family named John. Wonder what the father has to say about that?" So they asked Zechariah to write the name he wanted for the child.

When they handed him his writing tablet, Zechariah wrote with a flourish:

"His name is JOHN." And before they could get over their amazement, Zechariah found his voice again. "That's right. His name is John. What a wonderful blessing that God is allowing me to speak again!" He had other things to say too, thoughts he hadn't been able to express for nine months or so. Everybody was amazed as the story spread through the territory around.

"One thing is for sure," they said. "This child is bound to be something great because God's hand is in this."

Nobody was more certain of that than the father himself. All the ancient longing of his people he poured out in a poem (1:68-79) that said in effect:

"All the dreams of our old prophets are coming true. God has not forgotten Israel. A new powerful ruler from the house of David is going to save us from the hands of our enemies and make us free again. God is yet going to fulfill the promise made to father Abraham, that we will be able to serve God in holiness and righteousness forever!

"And you, child of ours, will be a prophet for God, one who will go before the Messiah to prepare the way. You will explain to the people what salvation involves and will call them to repentance so that God may forgive them. Then that great Day can come when the people who sit in darkness can have light, because people will know how to walk the way of peace."

So John grew spiritually strong, living out in the country without any publicity until the time came for him to begin his preaching.

Since *Mark* also has no birth or childhood stories about Jesus, Luke takes time to enter the stories he had heard told in various Christian groups three generations after the birth of Jesus. They are all tucked into *Luke*, chapter two. It was back in the time when Caesar Augustus was emperor of Rome, when he ordered the first census to be taken of the whole empire. Quirinius was governor of Syria. (No Roman record of such a census has been found. There was a census in Palestine when Quirinius was governor of Syria in 6 A.D. Somehow Luke's informers had hooked them up together as a reason for getting Joseph and Mary out of Nazareth and into Bethlehem where the "Savior" surely would be born.) Every man had to go to his hometown to sign up. Mary's husband, Joseph, chose to go back from Nazareth in Galilee all the way down to Bethlehem, the city where David was born, five miles south of Jerusalem. It's important to note that Joseph was a direct descendant of King David. And, even though she was pregnant, Mary had to make that trip with him.

That's where it happened. While they were there in Bethlehem, with no place to stay—even the Inn was full of overnight guests—she delivered the baby. Wrapping him warmly in cloth, she made an animal feeding trough into a makeshift cradle for him. (*Luke* 2:1-7)

Matthew also felt that some other birth stories, not found in *Luke*, should be added before the account of the ministry of Jesus as a man is told. That Gospel starts with a genealogy which puts Jesus in the family of David, and past David to Abraham. Even though the account later says (1:20) that Joseph had nothing to do with the conception of Jesus, it traces the lineage of Jesus through Joseph, not Mary. Readers familiar with the Old Testament will see many names they recognize in the list. The writer even comments that it is pretty neat that there were fourteen generations from Abraham to David, then fourteen from David to the deportation of Judah to Babylon, and now fourteen more from the exile of Babylon to the birth of Jesus. So Jesus is placed in the legal line of descent for a king of Judah.

"Mary presented Joseph with a real problem," Matthew says. "She was pregnant because of the Holy Spirit, but all Joseph knew was that she was pregnant and he did not do it. He loved her, but he was planning to break the marriage contract quietly so as not to embarrass her any more than necessary. It was then that an angel appears, but in a dream to Joseph instead of Mary. The angel assures Joseph that everything is on the up and up. The child is God's child and the boy's name is to be Jesus, for He will save the people from their sins," he explains.

"All this happens," Matthew decided, "in order to fulfill Old Testament prophecies. Isaiah had said that a young woman will conceive and bear a son who would remind everyone that God is with us (Emmanuel)."

Joseph woke up reassured and completed the marriage to Mary. The baby came and they followed the angel's instructions in naming him Jesus. *Matthew* gives no stories about Jesus' birth as *Luke* does, but picks up the story he had on file about an awesome event of about two years later.

Luke's story continued with the very night of the birth. Shepherds were out in nearby fields, he says, tending their flocks of sheep. Another angel-sighting is reported. An intensely bright light shone around them and when they froze with fear an unnamed angel used the regular opening words: "Don't be afraid. I am bringing you good news about a great joy that is coming to everybody: a Savior is being born in Bethlehem today, the Messiah of the Lord. You'll find him all wrapped up in cloth and lying in a manger."

That wasn't all. A whole chorus of angels were doing background music while the angel spoke:

"Glory to God in the highest, and on earth peace among Human Beings with whom God is pleased."

"This we have to see," the shepherds said to each other after the angels disappeared. "Let's get over to Bethlehem right away and see for ourselves."

Securing the sheep for the night, they hurried through the town until they found the stable where Mary and Joseph sat by the manger-cradle which held the new-born baby.

"It's true," they said. "It's just as the angel told us." And Mary and Joseph didn't seem surprised when the shepherds told them what had happened.

No revival meeting ever broke up with more shouting and singing than was heard in the streets of Bethlehem that night as the shepherds made their way back to the fields remembering all their Sabbath School lessons about how God would one day send a Savior for Israel!

As with John, there was only the eight-day wait until the baby boy was circumcised. There they formally gave him the name of Jesus. ("he shall save.") Then a month later (as prescribed in *Leviticus* 12) the parents were in Jerusalem for the ceremony of purifying the mother and of presenting their gift of two turtledoves or two pigeons for God's gift of their firstborn son. At the temple was an old man named Simeon, a very devout man who spent his time praying for the time when God would save Israel. The Holy Spirit had led him to believe that he would not die before he had seen God's Messiah. It was no accident that Simeon was there when Mary and Joseph came into the temple courtyard with the baby Jesus.

Trembling, he took the baby from the parents. Holding him high, he couldn't contain himself:

"Glory to God. Glory to God! Lord, You can let me die in peace now. I have seen with my own eyes this One You have prepared as a revelation to the

Gentiles and a Messiah for the people of Israel."

Turning to Mary, he continued:

"Look. This child is going to be the cause for both the rise and the fall of many in Israel. He will lay bare the hearts of people, and your own heart will be pierced with sorrow like a sword!"

It just so happened that another old timer was on the scene at the same time. Eighty-four-year-old Anna, long recognized as a prophetess, had practically lived in the temple for all the years since her husband had died. Night and day she prayed, often fasting as well, always hopeful that God would send a deliverer for her people. When she saw the baby she was moved to tell everyone that this boy would be the answer to her prayers.

Having performed all the religious duties associated with purifying the mother and dedicating the first son, Joseph and Mary then made their way back to their hometown of Nazareth where Jesus grew up. Strong in body, and maturing in wisdom beyond His years, Jesus grew with God's approval. (*Luke* 2:8-40)

While Luke's story now skips ahead twelve years, Matthew inserts his story of how the family moved from Bethlehem to Nazareth.

"Herod was king of Judea when some 'wise men' (probably astrologers who knew a lot about the movement of the planets and stars) came 'from the east' to Jerusalem. By the time *Matthew* is written, Jesus was acknowledged by many as "Master" all over the world. This story says that "wise men" could read of His coming greatness in the stars themselves. When they hit Jerusalem they began to ask where they could find the God-anointed son.

"Guess what we heard today?" some of Herod's security agents asked him.

"I have already heard it, and it disturbs me greatly," Herod replied. "I don't like talk about another king showing up. It gets people upset." (Afraid that the presence of his own sons and other relatives might get people 'upset,' Herod had ordered some of them executed recently.)

Not many hours had passed before the chief priests and scribes had been called into his court for a consultation.

"Where do the scriptures say that this 'Messiah' you talk about is to be born?" Herod asked bluntly.

There was only one place in their scripture that pinpointed the town, though many general references were made to some future "coming." The king wanted to get specific, so they quickly agreed that *Micah* 5:2 would have to be it.

"In Bethlehem of Judah," they answered. "The prophet, Micah, said 'You, O Bethlehem, are by no means the least among the rulers of Judah; from you is going to come a ruler who will govern My people of Israel.'"

That's all Herod wanted to know. He called in the "wise men" and found out what time they had first noticed the star that caught their attention. When they told him that their journey had been about two years building up, he was already building a horrible plan of his own.

"You men go on to Bethlehem and see if you can find this wonderful baby," he said in his most charming manner. "When you do, I will appreciate it if you will come back to tell me where he is, so I can go and worship him also."

Outside the city they hurried across the few miles to Bethlehem, and that night in David's city, the special star seemed straight overhead, a sure sign to them that they had arrived. Without any trouble they found the house where Mary and Joseph lived and gained admittance. There he was, the babe with the mother, the babe to whom the whole world would someday pay its homage. Their gifts would be the first tokens of His coming reign, gold, frankincense and myrrh. So gentiles as well as Jews would be drawn to His "kingdom."

With minds uneasy over what they knew of Herod's record for keeping promises, they followed a dream warning that they were in danger, so they left the country by a different route than they came, leaving the stage set for a massacre of innocent children by a jealous power-mad monarch.

Fortunately, Joseph was warned also in a dream:

"Don't waste a minute," an angel told him. "Get up right now and take Mary and Jesus and head out for Egypt. Herod is about to search this town for the child. Stay in Egypt until I give you further word."

Matthew has to pause to say: "This is what the prophet (*Hosea* 11:1) was talking about when he said 'Out of Egypt have I called My son.'" Obviously it wasn't, if you read the original text, but Matthew, like some preachers today, was not too careful with his "proof texts.")

"They've tricked me!" Herod shouted furiously when he heard that the visitors from the east had already left Bethlehem. "I can't trust anybody around here. Move the army into Bethlehem. I don't want any male child two years old or younger left alive in that town. That way I'll make sure I get this pretender to my throne!"

(Once again Matthew finds an Old Testament reference that seemed to him to be a prediction of this very event. At least the mood is correct. *Jeremiah* 31:15 says, "A loud wailing voice was heard in Ramah, Rachel weeping for her children, refusing to be consoled because they are no more.")

The story goes on. Herod dies, and the angel tells Joseph in another dream that it is safe to take the family back home. "Don't go back to Bethlehem;

Herod's son, Archelaus, is no better than he was. Go up into Galilee and settle in Nazareth." Some "prophet" must have said the Messiah would "be called a Nazarene," Matthew figured. (*Matthew* 2:1-23)

Anyway, we are ready now for the good news story about Jesus of Nazareth whose ministry begins with His association with John the Baptist. That we will pick up in chapter 3. But first *Luke* has a story about Jesus as a boy, the only one in the Gospel accounts.

"Every year at the feast of the Passover time, Jesus' parents made the pilgrimage to Jerusalem. The year Jesus was twelve they made the trip as usual. When the feast days were over they headed for home with the caravan of family and friends. The first night out on the road they discovered that Jesus was not in the procession. During the day they had just assumed that He was somewhere with relatives. It was too late now to go back to look for Him in the city, so they spent an anxious night camping with the other pilgrims. With first light the next day they were on their way. Jerusalem was a big city, and they checked every relative and friend they knew without success. Finally they went back to the temple and found Him sitting there with the teachers, asking them questions, weighing their answers, and sharing opinions of His own.

"Joseph and Mary could hardly believe it. Here was their son discussing religious questions with the leading teachers of the nation, and, what's more, the teachers seemed to be astonished at His information and understanding! Their sudden relief at finding him safe, as well as their surprise at discovering Him in this unusual situation, issued in a perfectly natural parental question:

"'Son, why have You treated us this way?' "It was Mary who spoke. "Your father and I have been looking everywhere for you."

"Oh, mother, didn't you know I would be here in my Father's house?"

It was a word and an experience that Mary would never forget during the next few years as Jesus showed Himself to be the perfectly caring and obedient son in their home in Nazareth.

And again Luke repeats what he said about Jesus (verse 40) before he added the story about the experience in the temple, "Jesus grew up physically and intellectually developing good relationships both with God and other people." (2:52)

The Time Has Come

Meanwhile, the time came for God to move John into action. He had grown up in the "wilderness" region near the Jordan River and was ready when the Lord spoke. If you don't read the first two verses of Luke's chapter 3 too quickly, the awesome impact of what he is saying hits you. It tells of "the word of the Lord" coming to somebody.

"In the fifteenth year of the reign of Tiberius Caesar," the long sentence begins. Who was Tiberius Caesar? Just the supreme emperor of the Roman world, that's all. If the Lord was going to speak to somebody, why not the top person? But there is only a little comma after his name. Well, if you are moving down to the provincial level of government, how about speaking to the governor? ". . . Pontius Pilate being governor of Judea," another comma, or at least one of the three tetrarchs who governed about a third of Palestine each, "Herod being tetrarch of Galilee (comma), and his brother Phillip, tetrarch of the region of Ituraea and Trachonitis (comma), and Lysanius tetrarch of Abilene (comma). . ."

Well, of course, God may not speak through the heads of state, but surely the word would come through the heads of Church. The sentence continues, ". . . in the high priesthood of Annas and Caiaphas, (just another comma) the word of God came to WHOM? . . . to John, the son of Zechariah in the wilderness!" Of all that list of important people, was John the only one listening?

And when the word came, John went. All up and down the Jordan region John went preaching that God was calling for people to repent of their sins and be baptized as a sign they were serious about it. The prophet Isaiah had dreamed of this day (*Isaiah* 40:3-6) when "the voice of one crying in the wilderness would call for the way of the Lord to be prepared. 'Fill every valley; level off every mountain; make all the crooked roads straight, and make all the rough roads smooth, so that all living things shall see the salvation of God!'"

People who saw John had no trouble recognizing him. He wore clothes made out of camel's hair, with a large leather girdle around his waist. At lunch time he snacked on locusts and wild honey. (*Matthew* 3:4)

People who heard John had no trouble figuring out what he was saying. When they flocked down from the cities to hear the sensational preacher, he greeted them with remarks like these:

"You bunch of snakes! Who warned you to flee from the coming judgment. You are great at saying 'We have Abraham for our father, so the Lord will always save us.' If God ever lacks for children of Abraham, God can raise up some more from these stones. No, you had better concentrate on doing right and acting like children of God. Judgment time is here for our nation. The ax is ready to cut down every tree that doesn't bear good fruit."

That got them excited. "What shall we do? Tell us what to do!"

"All right, I'll be specific. If you have two coats, share one with a person who has none. If you have food and someone else is hungry, share your food. That's serving God."

Tax collectors asked "What about us?" John was

right to the point: "Don't collect any more than you are supposed to. Be honest."

Soldiers asked, "And what shall we do?"

"Don't rob anyone by force, or by falsely accusing them of something. Be content with your wages."

Somehow they had expected something a little more "religious."

"Who is this man?" the people began asking. "Is this the Messiah?"

John laid that rumor to rest by saying publicly "I am one who baptizes you with water, but another one mightier than I is coming. I am not worthy to untie his shoelaces. He will baptize you with the Holy Spirit and fire. His judgment will be like the harvester who winnows out the grain to save in the granary, and the chaff he will burn up." (*Luke* 3:1-17), also (*Matthew* 3:7-12)

Unfortunately, John's popular ministry was to be cut short. Herod, the tetrarch, was criticized soundly by John for taking his own brother's wife, Herodias, and for a number of other misdeeds that were public record. Herod retaliated by locking John up in prison. Before he did, however, Jesus had a chance to visit him. In fact, He wanted John to baptize Him along with the others who accepted his invitation.

"I need to be baptized by You," John said to Jesus. "You don't need to come to me."

"No, let it be this way for now; it doesn't hurt any of us to do these things that show Whose side we are on." With that as Jesus' reply, John went through with the ceremony. Such an intense experience it was for Jesus that as He was praying at the edge of the water following his baptism He was conscious of the Spirit of God like a dove descending on Him. He heard an inner voice saying: "You are my dearly loved Son, and I am well pleased with you." (*Matthew* 4:13-17, *Mark* 1:9-11, *Luke* 4:21-22)

(Because Luke had plunged right into his story at the beginning, he now has to pause long enough to put his version of the Jesus' family tree into the record, just as Matthew did before he started his account. Matthew's starts with Abraham and works down to Jesus. Luke's starts with Jesus and works back to Abraham, and then on back to Adam and the original Parent, God. Both emphasize Jesus' descent from the great King David. However, Luke's informant says that Joseph's line from David came through one of David's sons named Nathan, while Matthew traces Joseph's lineage back to David through Solomon. Evidently the Christian churches didn't care to argue the point, so both genealogies were left in the books.)

Following the exciting experience at His baptism, Jesus had to get away by Himself and think. If He were going to be God's chosen One Who would bring God's Spirit rule to earth, He faced several tremendous questions. This was a time for meditation and prayer. So He went out by Himself to the desert country near the river and stayed for days. His mind was so intent on discovering the will of God for His life that He did not even take time to eat. There in the wilderness He went through His whole message and mission.

Both Matthew and Luke take the two verses of *Mark* 1:12-13 and expand the report to give details that Jesus must have passed on to His followers later when He was telling how God led Him through three specific issues He had to face.

When He realized He was hungry, the thought, prompted by the Evil One and not by God, came to Him that maybe He could use His God-given power to turn the little stones that looked like loaves of bread into real bread. All people need bread, and He could certainly gain many followers by furnishing bread for them too. But He answered that thought with another from the scripture: (Scriptural advice is an excellent way to answer that basic H.B. temptation to turn the "I" into Number 1.)

"No person lives by bread alone, but by the life-giving Word of God!"

A second great temptation came also. Matthew puts it second; Luke puts it third; the order doesn't matter. In His imagination He was led to the temple in Jerusalem and saw Himself standing on the very top of the tower. "What a spectacular show it would make if You would jump off and then have God's angels catch You just before You hit the ground. With God's Spirit with You, You wouldn't even bruise Your foot!" So the devilish inner voice whispered. But Jesus knew that when a leader starts doing the spectacular in order to get people's attention there is no end to the process; they want more and bigger spectaculars. He would need to change people, not amaze them. Even deeper than that, the realization came again from His reading of scripture: "You shall not tempt the Lord your God by asking God to do something special for You that God doesn't do for everyone else."

"Perhaps the end justifies the means," Jesus also thought as He turned the question over and over in His mind: "How do I get in a position powerful enough to change the world society into the kind of social order God approves? If I will use the kind of power and coercion the devil does and get economic and military and political control over the nations, then I can use my great power to help people and teach them the Way of the Lord.

"Meanwhile, I would have become one who is serving the devil rather than God! No, I will have to use God's methods to attain God's goals. I can never compromise the Way of Love. But those temptations to save myself, or to serve myself, or to get power and privilege for myself still are ready to beckon when the time is right. The devil in us never gives up." (*Matthew* 4:1-11; *Luke* 4:1-13)

It was about that time that John was arrested by Herod, and Jesus had to make His move. He came into Galilee preaching the message of which He had become sure in the desert retreat:

"At last the time has come; the kingdom of God has arrived. You must be ready to change your heart and mind and believe the good news that God's Spirit is ruling now. You don't have to wait any longer; you can live NOW in God's Presence."

Immediately people turned the kind of attention they had been giving to John to Jesus. Everywhere in Galilee they invited Him to speak in their synagogues, and everywhere He went He was a big "hit."

Word of His success got back to His hometown of Nazareth, of course. And when they heard that Jesus was coming home for a visit, the synagogue was filled to overflowing on the sabbath because He still held to His family custom of participating in the synagogue service of worship and discussion every week. Sure enough, He came. So the synagogue leader invited Him to read the part of the scripture which lay people read each sabbath. Jesus accepted the invitation, went to the front of the hall, found the place in the scroll of *Isaiah* (61:1-2) and began to read:

"The Spirit of the Lord is upon Me, because the Lord has anointed Me to bring good tidings to the poor and afflicted; God has sent Me to heal the brokenhearted, to proclaim liberty to the captives and the recovering of sight to the blind, to make oppressed people free, and to tell of the Lord's coming rule."

Then He closed the book, without adding as *Isaiah* did '. . .and the day of vengeance of our God.'

Everyone just stared at Him as He handed the book back to the attendant and sat down again. He didn't have to speak loudly to be heard:

"Today this scripture reading has been fulfilled in your hearing." Then He went on to say what He thought the prophet meant, and the people were amazed that their hometown boy had developed into such an eloquent teacher. Yet only a few believed He could heal them. The rest hung back as some began to talk among themselves:

"Who would ever have thought that Joseph's son would ever have been anything more than our carpenter? Where did He get so great? . . .Why, I've known His family for years before He was born!" (*Mark* and *Matthew* add: "Isn't this Mary's son, and aren't His brothers, James, Joses, Simon, and Judah, and all His sisters still living here?")

And understanding what they were whispering or thinking, Jesus brought it out in the open. "You may be thinking of the familiar proverb: 'Physician, heal yourself,' because you would like to see Me do some of the miraculous things you've heard I did in Capernaum. But, you know, it is also true that no prophet is acceptable in his own country. You remember the stories of Elijah, when the great drought was on the land and it didn't rain for three and a half years. Famine was everywhere, and there were a lot of needy widows in Israel. But Elijah was sent by the Lord to none of them, only to the widow named Zarephath in Sidon. And there were many lepers in Israel in the time of Elisha, but not one of them was cured, only the Syrian, Naaman."

He may as well have said "You don't have the faith or the understanding here to accept God's help through me." That's the way they took it anyway, so they pushed Him out of the synagogue. By the time they hit the street, the congregation had turned into a mob and some were even trying to throw Him over the cliff on which part of the city was built. But Jesus ended up walking right through the disorganized crowd and out of His hometown forever. (*Luke* 4:14-30)

There were others, however, who thought so highly of Him that they changed their whole life pattern in order to follow Him. Both *Mark* (1:19-20) and *Matthew* (4:18-22) tell of the first of them.

One day as He was walking along the shore of the lake of Galilee, He saw two fishermen, Simon and his brother Andrew, throwing their nets into the water. They had been disciples of John and had, no doubt, followed closely Jesus' beginning career.

"Come and follow me," Jesus called out to them, "and I will teach you to catch people instead of fish."

They pulled up their nets and put them away. Their decision was made and they went with Him. A little farther along the shore they saw the Zebedee boys, James and John. They were on board a large fishing boat with their father and some hired men mending nets. Jesus invited those brothers also to go along with Him, and they too left their fishing business immediately.

The little group went into the town where Jesus made His headquarters, Capernaum, and on the first Sabbath day after returning Jesus went to the synagogue where He was guest teacher of the adult class. Everyone was used to hearing the Scribes who were the regular teachers. They could quote what was in the holy books, but Jesus talked on His own authority. The people were amazed.

Right in the middle of the lesson, a crazy man came running into the synagogue yelling at the top of his voice:

"What are You doing here, Jesus of Nazareth? Are You going to kill me? I know who You are; You're God's special representative!"

Jesus stopped him with these sharp words, "Shut up and get out of him!"

At that time everyone thought that when a person was mentally ill or physically sick it was because an evil spirit had gone to live inside him or her, so Jesus spoke as if He were talking to the evil spirit inside the man, not to the man himself.

Somehow the command got through to the man's real mind. He shuddered as if a tremendous struggle was going on inside himself, then let out one loud scream. That was all. The man had returned to normal and his mind was back on the right track.

Everyone in the synagogue was so astounded that they kept saying to each other, "What on earth happened? This man is not only teaching with authority, but when He gives orders even the evil spirits obey Him!"

After that the tales about Jesus spread like wildfire all through Galilee. (*Mark* 1:21-28; *Luke* 4:31-37)

Immediately following the morning session in the synagogue, Jesus, with James and John, went home with Simon and Andrew who lived in Capernaum. Peter's mother-in-law was sick in bed with a high fever, and the other people in the house told Jesus about it the first thing. He went into the room, took her by the hand and helped her to her feet. Immediately, the fever left her and she felt so well that she went right to work preparing a meal for them.

Now the whole town was excited. Before evening they were coming from all over Capernaum bringing their sick people to Him for healing. Everybody in town was trying to get into Simon Peter's yard, and Jesus did heal a great number of people who were suffering from various ailments. *Mark* and *Luke* add that the demons knew full well they were dealing with the holy Son of God. *Matthew* saw it all as fulfilling another statement from *Isaiah* (53:4) that said God's Special Man would "take our infirmities and bear our diseases." (*Mark* 1:29-34; *Matthew*

8:14-17; *Luke* 4:38-41)

Very early the next morning, while it was still dark, Jesus got up, left the house and went out onto a hill outside of town. There He found a spot to pray. When Simon and the others got up in the morning and found that He had gone, they went out looking for Him. Later that morning when they found Him, they said, "Everybody is looking for You."

"In that case we had better go on to the other towns around the shore," Jesus replied. "I have to preach my message there too, for I should not spend all my time in one place."

So they moved on through the other towns of Galilee, preaching in their synagogues and healing lots of sick people. One day a man with leprosy came up and knelt down before Jesus and pled for help:

"If You want to, You can make me well."

Jesus felt so sorry for the man that He reached out and put His hand on his head and said, "Of course I want to. You are well." Everybody looked and realized that the man actually was cured of his leprosy. Then Jesus gave the man this instruction:

"Before you talk about this everywhere, I want you to do one thing. Go straight from here and show yourself to the priest, the way our scripture commands you. Let him examine you and declare officially that you are well. That way everybody will be satisfied that you no longer have leprosy. There you can make the offering Moses once prescribed for one who is healed, in *Leviticus* 14."

But the man who was healed couldn't keep quiet. He talked a lot to everybody he saw about what Jesus had done, and the story spread far and wide. The thing that Jesus feared would happen did happen. It became impossible for Him to show His face inside a town because of the crowds of people who pressed about Him with only one thing in mind—to be cured of some illness. He tried to camp out with His disciples in some lonely places, but even out in the countryside people found Him, and the crowds gathered around Him every day. They came from as far as Tyre and Sidon on the west and the region beyond the Jordan River on the east. (*Mark* 1:35-45; *Matthew* 4:23-25; *Luke* 4:42-44)

One was a woman who for eighteen years she had been unable to straighten up. Jesus saw her all bent over in a synagogue one Sabbath where He was teaching. Moving over to where she was, He put His hands on her and said, "Woman, you are now free of whatever has bound your spirit and your body. Stand up straight!"

Her body straightened and the joyful emotion of the moment prompted her to cry out her praises to God. All the people were amazed, but the head of the synagogue did not join the celebration of her freedom. Instead, indignant because Jesus had done this in the middle of a Sabbath service, he called out to the people:

"There are six days of every week when work is to be done. You can come on any one of those days and be healed. But this is not allowed on the Sabbath day."

Jesus turned on him and other synagogue leaders who nodded in agreement.

"You hypocrites! Every Sabbath, doesn't every one of you untie his ox or his donkey from its stall and take it to water? Of course you do. Shouldn't this woman, one of our own Hebrew family, who has been bound by Satan for eighteen years, be untied from her bonds on the Sabbath day?"

In their embarrassment, the leaders did not answer, but the people cheered for Jesus. The answer to the question was evident to them. (*Luke* 13:10-17)

On another sabbath Jesus faced a similar situation

when He was eating dinner with prominent Pharisees at the home of one of their number. One man in the group had limbs swollen with dropsy. Seeing what distress he was in, Jesus asked the Pharisees present whether it was lawful to heal on the sabbath or not.

Nobody answered. So Jesus healed the man, then commented to them all, "If one of you had an ox or a donkey that had fallen into a well, wouldn't you pull it out on the sabbath?" (*Luke* 14:1-6)

There was a report going around that the Roman governor, Pilate, had ordered his soldiers to attack a crowd of Jews while they were offering sacrifices in the temple. Some, including fellow Galileans of Jesus, died there. Jesus took the opportunity to comment on the popular idea that misfortune always comes to those who sin:

"Do you think that these Galileans who were killed were worse sinners than others of our people? I tell you they were not. But one thing is sure, unless you all give up your acts of rebellion against Rome and concentrate on the kingdom of God, you will all suffer the same fate one day. You have been saying, too, that the eighteen people killed when the tower in Siloam fell must have been worse sinners than other people in Jerusalem. Wrong again! But unless you repent tragedy will strike our whole nation.

"It is not that God wants our nation to perish, but how long can we get away with ignoring God's plan for us? A man had a fig tree planted in his orchard, but he never found any fruit on it. One day he said to his gardener, 'Look, I've been checking this tree for three years and I have never found any fruit on it. It's just wasting space; let's cut it down.' The gardener wanted to give it another chance. 'Let's leave it one more year. I'll fertilize it and give it extra care, and if it bears next year it will be worth the effort. If it doesn't, we can cut it down.'" (*Luke* 13:1-9)

(We are in that fourth year now, God's Gardener was saying.)

Luke had a more detailed story of Jesus' calling the four fishermen to be His disciples. Here he tells his story:

"One of those times when the people were pressing all around Him, He had to get into a fishing boat in order to have a place from which to speak to the crowd. There were two boats pulled up to the edge of the calm lake while the fishermen were washing their nets. It was Simon Peter's boat Jesus got into. Simon was nearby, so He asked him to put the boat out just a little way from the shore so He could be seen and heard by everyone. When He was through with the lecture, Jesus turned to Simon and suggested that they move out into the deep water and put down the nets for another try for fish.

"Teacher, we worked all night here and took absolutely nothing, but if You say so I will try it one more time." With that remark, Simon moved out and let the nets down again.

"Wait a minute. . ." Simon and Andrew both started to exclaim at the same time. "We've got more than we can handle! This catch is bursting our net!" With both hands busy, they called to their partners in the other boat, "Come on out here quick and help us hold them."

By the time they had worked the boats back to the shore, both boats were full of fish. But busy as he was, Simon Peter was thinking deeply. As soon as the boats were secured, he fell down at Jesus' knees and said, "Master, You had better leave me; I am a sinful man." Andrew, James and John all nodded as if to include themselves in Peter's expression of not being worthy to be there with Jesus. And, according to Luke, that's when Jesus said to them, "Don't be afraid. From now on you will be catching people." (*Luke* 5:1-11)

That was the day they parked their boats and left their fishing business to accompany Jesus on His preaching and teaching tours.

We are not told all the places Jesus went, nor all the things He said, but the Gospel writers tried to fit together in an order that seemed best to each of them the important pieces of information they had as they wrote at least 35 years after Jesus' crucifixion. Both *Matthew* and *Luke* think it is time right here to put in a summary of some of Jesus' key teachings.

Words To Live By

One of the times when Jesus left the crowds and went out into the hills to pray, His disciples gathered around Him and He gave them enough to remember that Matthew's readers would call it "The Sermon on the Mount." The collection begins with a list of "Good Attitudes" that make for good life.

"It is the humble minded who put their whole trust in God instead of themselves who are really fortunate, for the kingdom of heaven belongs to them.

"The people who mourn for the sin of the world, and for their own sin, will be able to receive real comfort themselves.

"The people who do not strike out in anger because their trust is in the judgment of God will have the strength to win out in the end.

"The people who want to do right as much as a hungry or thirsty person wants food and drink will be filled with the spirit of Life.

"The people who are sympathetically merciful to others will have mercy shown to them.

"The people whose motives are pure in wanting fellowship with God will know God.

"The people who try to build right relationships between all persons will be known as children of God because they are doing God's work.

"Even if those people have to suffer rejection or persecution because they are true to God and are working to make righteousness prevail, they are joyful because they know themselves to be part of the kingdom of heaven.

"And so it will be with you," He added pointedly to those new disciples. "When people make fun of you, or tell lies about you, or even hurt you because of your partnership with me, be glad of it. You will find your reward in heaven, and here you will share the experience of the great prophets of the past, all of whom were persecuted in some manner." (*Matthew* 5:1-12)

Luke wrote some of these same "beatitudes," only with a different twist. It could well be that Jesus Himself turned His phrases differently at different times to fit the theme of His teaching on different occasions. Instead of giving "mountaintop" spiritual expressions as principles on which disciples should base their lives, as in *Matthew* 5, *Luke* reports Jesus speaking "on a level place" (6:17), right down on the level with poor and sick and troubled people of every sort, Jews and gentiles alike. Here He was the exhorter urging them to hang in there and trust God.

"You poor people are actually blessed; the kingdom of God belongs to you. God is on your side.

"You people who are hungry now will have enough to eat when God's rule is realized on earth.

"You who are crying now with sorrow will one day be laughing with joy!

"And, I tell you, when other people despise you and throw you out of their society because you try to live what I am teaching, you can actually leap for joy. That's the way their ancestors reacted to all the prophets we now honor. Besides, the reward we are going to get in life to come will more than make up for all the garbage we have to put up with now.

"But the rich people can be warned; they are getting their consolation and rewards now, but they can't take it with them. The people who have more than enough now will go hungry later. The people who are so comfortable and happy now will one day mourn and cry. And if everybody speaks well of you because you are not saying or doing anything with which they disagree, just think! That puts you on the side of the false prophets who were popular when God's real prophets were persecuted."

"Just what does a true disciple do in the "real" world of today? Spell that out for us, Jesus." Luke could almost hear the disciples and others asking for specifics. So in His account, Jesus continues:

"I'll tell you plainly what I mean. Love your enemies; do good to those who hate you. When people curse you, you bless them. When people abuse you, you pray for them. If someone hits you on one cheek, turn the other one to give him or her the chance to hit you again. If someone takes your overcoat from you, offer that person your jacket as well. When anyone begs something of you, give it. If somebody takes something of yours, don't ask for it back.

"And the underlying rule of it all is this: you do to other people what you would want them to do to you.

"You see, it works like this. If you only love those who love you, what virtue is in that? Even people who are not trying to be godly do that. And if you only do good to people who do good to you, what's so great about that? Everybody lives up to that level of action. If you are willing to lend to someone from whom you know you are going to be repaid, you aren't risking anything at all. Anybody will do that. But if you love your enemies, or do something good to your enemy, or lend to someone in need and expect nothing in return, then you will have moved up to the level of the real children of God. You will then be acting exactly as God acts with us, because God is kind and considerate even to the most ungrateful and selfish of us. We ought to show the same kind of caring for others in our human family that our heavenly Parent has for us all." (*Luke* 6:17-36)

Back to *Matthew* now, Jesus said that people who try to live these attributes of divine love are really "the salt of the earth," the people who preserve the good and make life tasteful. "But," He added, "if salt loses its saltiness, what good is it? How do you season salt? It's not good for anything then; it gets thrown out. Be careful that you don't get stale.

"Or you might think of yourselves as light for the world. You will be noticed, because a city sitting on a hilltop can't be hid. Light is for shining anyway. People don't light a lamp and then put it under a bushel basket to hide it. They put it on a lampstand so that it can give light in the house. So make sure that your lighted life shines so people can see it, and then when they see these good things you do they will give credit to God Who is the source of our light! (*Matthew* 5:13-16, *Luke* 14:34-35 is similar.)

"I know that these instructions I am giving you are not exact quotations from the Law and the Prophets which we accept as scripture, but you can see that I am not trying to throw the old scripture away; I am trying to fill them with meaning for today. The basic laws laid down in the scripture are not yet fulfilled; we can't relax the moral requirements it makes upon us, and anyone who says we should is least helpful in bringing in the kingdom of heaven. But, I tell you, the person who not only teaches them but lives them out fully will be most important in establishing the kingdom of heaven. You see, your righteousness has got to go beyond keeping the letter of the law, as the scribes and Pharisees try to do. You have to live in the spirit of the laws of God, which is nothing else than love, or you will never get inside that love relationship that is God's order of life.

"Let me illustrate:

"One of the old laws (*Exodus* 20:13 and *Deuteronomy* 24:1) says 'You shall not kill; and whoever kills shall be liable to the judgment.' But I am saying that everyone who is angry with another person is already on dangerous ground. Whoever insults another person is already breaking the spirit of the law, although no council can easily judge the intention of the heart. Words can "kill" too. Whoever calls another a fool is in danger that your burning anger will become hell for yourself. In fact, keeping this desire for good relationships with other people perfectly clear and open is so important that you should think of it first even when you are bringing a gift to the altar of the church. If you remember there that someone has something against you, then leave the altar and go to that person and try to make things right between you. Then you can come back and finish your worship.

"If there is still some dispute between you, make every effort to settle it before it goes to court. If it is a matter of owing a debt, settle it out of court because the judge will only make you pay, and you may spend time in jail as well!" (Also *Luke* 12:57-59)

"Another one of the old laws said that 'you should not commit adultery.' I am saying to you that when a man looks at a woman lustfully he has already committed adultery with her in his heart. It is not just the outward acts that involve other people that affect a person; the inner thought or desire also affects him or her. What you see, what you do, and where you go all help shape your character, your real self. I know this is overstating the case, but if what you keep looking at is causing you to sin, then you'd be better off to pull your eye out. You can better afford to lose an eye than to give your attention to something that may cause you to lose your inner life. If what you are doing or making is tearing down your spiritual self, then you would be healthier to cut off your hand and quit doing what you are doing. If your feet are following a path that involves you in a dishonest or hurtful way of life, then cut off your foot. Better to go limping into heaven than to run swiftly into hell! Allowing yourself to harden into a bad character could condemn you to living forever in the hell of your own making." (*Matthew* 5:17-30; *Mark* 9:43-48)

(This admonition not to take lightly our own responsibility for our own personal life growth evidently was something Jesus stressed more than once. *Matthew* repeats this eye, hand and foot saying again in 18:8-9.)

"Here's another illustration. The old Law (*Deuteronomy* 24:1) also says that a man can divorce his wife simply by giving her a written notice. But what is he doing to her? As far as she is concerned she is still keeping her side of the marriage covenant. But now she must go to another husband in order to have a home, and so she is now committing adultery, in a strict sense, and it is her former husband who forced her to do it. He also puts the man who now marries her in the same position. The man who keeps only the letter of this divorce law may still be violating God's intention for marriage." (*Matthew* 5:31-32; *Luke* 16:18)

Mark 10:11-12 simply puts it: "Whoever divorces his wife and marries another commits adultery, and the same goes for the woman who divorces her husband to marry another."

"Maybe it is time," Jesus is saying, "that we fill out the old Law to consider the rights of the woman involved in marriage as well as the man. Here's another instance where my followers will have to live above the law.

"'And there are many more, like swearing oaths. . .The old law said that 'You shall not swear falsely, and so profane the Name of the Lord.' (*Leviticus* 19:12) But I ask you, "Why swear at all? Some people say 'I swear by heaven'; others say 'I swear by Jerusalem, the Holy City'; and others say 'I swear by my head.' But all these belong to God, and God doesn't think that swearing in any of these ways, or any other, will make the truth more truthful. Just tell the truth and let your word stand on its own merit. 'Yes' or 'No' is good enough without any embellishment if you are truthful." (*Matthew* 5:33-37)

"'Another old law, found in all three of the law books, *Exodus* 21:24, *Leviticus* 24:30, and *Deuteronomy* 19:21, is popular still: 'An eye for an eye and a tooth for a tooth!' I am saying that we should go beyond that. You don't have to hit back when someone hits you. You don't have to fight back legally when somebody sues you to take away something from you. Give him more and see what he thinks of that! If a soldier forces you to carry his pack one mile, which is the legal limit, take it an extra mile for him and see how that makes him feel!". . .And so Matthew's account continues here with the same ideas we noted in Luke's sixth chapter: "Don't refuse someone who wants to borrow from you. . .love your enemies because God sends rain on the unjust person's farm just as well as the good person's. . .After all, our goal must be to be as perfectly loving and caring as God is!" (*Matthew* 5:38-48)

"You must understand that the point of all that we do or don't do is to be found in the kind of persons we become ourselves. So be careful that you don't make a show of your religious life in order to get approval from other people. You may get that, but you won't get any real satisfaction in knowing that you have God's approval.

"When you give your offerings, don't make a big show of your giving so everybody can applaud your generosity. Hypocrites who do that already have their reward when they have the praise of other people. But you should be so intent on giving to help others and to show your appreciation for what God has given you that your left hand doesn't even keep a record of what your right hand is giving. Your giving will be in secret, but God will see and will reward you appropriately.

"The same thing is true with your praying. You don't want to be like the show-offs who love to stand and pray in public so people can see how pious and godly they are. They want others to notice them, and that is all the reward they get—the notice of others. But when you pray, go into your room and shut the door and pray where no one knows you are praying. That way you will know whether you are honestly wanting to communicate with God personally. God will know your heart, and will deal with you accordingly. There, in private, you won't need to repeat a lot of empty phrases, the way some public pray-ers do. Some people think that the more words a prayer has the better it is. But God already knows what you need even before you pray. You aren't trying to bend God to your will; you are trying to discover God's will and then to find the strength and insight to line up with it." (*Matthew* 6:1-8)

"If you want a sort of model to keep in mind when you pray, think like this:

Matthew 6:9-13

"Our Father, God of
heaven,
May Your Name be
honored.
May Your kingdom

Luke 11:2-4

"Father,
Your Name be honored
and Your kingdom come.
Give us each day the
bread we need;

come, and
Your will be done
On earth as it is in heaven
Give us today just the bread we need,
And forgive us for obligations to You which we have not fulfilled, as we forgive others who have not kept their obligations to us.
Let us not be tested too sorely when evil days come.''

And forgive us our sins because we forgive everyone who is indebted to us.
Keep us from falling to temptation.''

''I can't stress too much the truth that if you do not forgive other people their unmet obligations to you, then God cannot forgive you for yours. If you do forgive others, your own spirit will be open to receive God's forgiveness.'' (*Matthew* 6:14-15; *Mark* 11:25- 26)

''One other thing (since ''fasting'' was one of the big three religious acts to be performed by devout Jews of Jesus' day), apply this same principle of secrecy in order to keep your motive pure when you practice fasting. Many religious hypocrits make sure everyone knows they are giving up food by marking their faces and looking sad and solemn. So having people know that is all the reward they will get. But you, when you fast, clean up, and act natural in every way so that no one will know except God. Your reward, then, will come from God, not from people.'' (*Matthew* 6:16-18)

''Keep in mind always what kind of reward or treasure you are after in this world. Think about what happens when you spend your life storing up things you ''own.'' Moths can eat your good clothes; rust and wear can eat your physical assets; thieves can steal it all. But spiritual treasures of character and relationships are out of the reach of natural elements and thieves. So, be careful what you desire most, because where your treasure is your heart will be also." (*Matthew* 6:19-21)

The same point was stressed again when someone in the crowd of followers asked Jesus "Won't You tell my brother to divide our family inheritance with me?"

"No," Jesus replied, "I'm not the one who should settle your financial affairs. But I will tell you and everyone here that you should be on your guard against any inclination to covet what someone else possesses, because a person's life is not to be measured by the quantity of his/her possessions.

"A rich man had good land which produced such a big crop one year that he didn't know where to store it all. 'What am I going to do now?' he wondered. Then he said to himself, 'I know what I'll do; I'll tear down my old barns and build larger ones. Then I will have room to store all my stuff, and I'll be on easy street for years. I can just eat, drink and be merry; nothing to worry about now.'

"But God said to him 'You're a fool! When you die tonight who is going to get all these things you have prepared?'

"That's the way it is with a person who tries to lay up treasures for himself and doesn't make sure that he cultivates spiritual riches from God which last forever." (*Luke* 12:13-21)

More of the same emphasis came in another story.

Inside the big house the rich man ate gourmet meals every day and dressed in the latest fashions. Outside, by the back gate a poor beggar named Lazarus lay every day. He was sick and had sores all over his body; he would have been content just to get the scraps from the rich man's table. His only companions were the dogs that came and licked his sores. Finally the poor man died and was ushered by angels into the presence of father Abraham in heaven.

Later the rich man died also. His destination was hell, and part of the torment of hell was that he could see into the heaven he had missed. There he could see Lazarus embraced by Abraham.

"Father Abraham," he called out, "show mercy to me. Send Lazarus to me to give me a drink. Just let him dip his finger in the water and cool my tongue; I'm burning up." (Was the former rich man still thinking that Lazarus ought to serve him?)

Abraham, with godly concern, still recognized the tormented man as a member of the family. "Son, I'm sorry. Remember that in your lifetime on earth you had all the good things while Lazarus suffered all the bad; but now he is enjoying life here while you are in misery. The problem is that there is such a gulf between heaven and hell that no one can cross over."

"Then let Lazarus go back to our home where my five brothers still live. . ." the rich man was still trying to plot an arrangement that would bring some profit out of this situation. . ."and let him warn them so they won't end up here too."

"No," Abraham had to answer, "they have Moses and the prophets (and now Jesus); let them pay attention to them."

"Oh no, father Abraham, don't you see that if someone goes to them from the dead, they will listen and repent!"

"Unfortunately," Abraham closed the conversation, "if they won't listen to Moses and the prophets, they won't be convinced even if someone did rise from the dead." (*Luke* 16:19-31)

"Actually," *Luke* 12:33 says, "when you exchange your possessions for gifts to share with other people who are in need, you are simply transferring your assets to the heavenly bank that never fails!

"What gets your attention gets you. If your eye is seeing clearly, the way of life is plain to you. If your eye is looking at darkness instead of light, your whole life will be dark. Give your full attention to seeing God's Way and your whole life will be full of light.

"You can't look two ways at once, just as no one can serve two masters finally. You must end up serving one and ignoring the other. You can't serve both God and money or material things.

"You have to choose, and I am telling you that you ought not to give first-place importance to material possessions. Don't be so worried about the physical trappings of your life, your food and your clothes. They certainly can't be the most important things in life. Birds that don't worry one bit about their food discover that God sees that they are fed. You are worth more than birds, aren't you? Will worry add one day to your life span, or one inch to your stature? But you worry, too, about how you dress. The flowers of the field don't do one bit of work or worry about clothing, but God dresses them pretty well, don't you think? Even King Solomon, in all his glorious array, was not dressed as beautifully as the little flowers. Now, if God puts the right fashion on the grass of the field which lasts only a few days before it is burned in an oven, won't God take care of you?

"What shall we eat? What shall we drink? What shall we wear?. . .These are the things people worry about when they don't know of the God Who cares for us! Don't give your first-place attention to them. Make the kingdom of God and its way of right living the A-1 priority in your life, and then all these other things you really need will take their place in your life as well.

"So, stop worrying about the future. Don't borrow

trouble from tomorrow. Tomorrow will have enough troubles of its own. Today is the tomorrow you worried about yesterday. Just do your best to live today as best you can." (*Matthew* 6:22-37; *Luke* 11:34-36; 16:13; 12:22-31)

On the other hand, it's not wise to let today be ruled by yesterday either. Maybe that's why *Matthew* puts Jesus' remarks about "judging" immediately after His advice that we not worry about tomorrow. Because judgment chains to the past if we aren't careful. (I don't have to think about you today because I already decided yesterday that you are no good.) A "judgmental" attitude that makes me quick to judge or even prejudge others can get me into trouble if other people start using that same unforgiving attitude in judging me. I may start being measured the same way I am measuring others. Sooner or later, it will in fact work out that way, Jesus says.

"Almost invariably when we condemn others we overlook similar faults in ourselves. Why do you notice a tiny speck in your neighbor's eye and can't see a log in your own eye? And yet we are quick to say 'Let me take that speck out of your eye.' Who is the hypocrite now? First, give your attention to correcting your own faults, taking the log out of your own eye, then you may be able to see clearly enough to help your sister or brother work on that person's fault. And you will be a lot more sympathetic and patient as you do!" (*Matthew* 7:1-5; *Luke* 6:37-38, 41-42)

Perhaps to make sure that we see clearly that Jesus is condemning the judgmental attitude, and not saying that we never have to make judgments about anybody or anything, *Matthew* 7:6 is added. "You have to use common sense. You wouldn't give dogs what is holy, and you wouldn't throw your pearls in front of pigs thinking they would be careful in their treatment of them. You could expect pigs to trample them, and perhaps still turn to attack you.

"But remember that while judgment chains to the past, prayer looks to the future. Instead of judging people, pray for them. Instead of worrying about tomorrow, pray for God to give you what you need for life, and then leave the matter with God.

"Just ask, and you will be given what you need; seek, and you will find the truth you are searching for; knock, and doors of opportunity will open to you. Life is set up by God so the questioner finds answers, the seeker discovers truth, and the persistent door-knocker will finally get to enter. You know why? Because God is a parent like some of you. If your little child asks for a small loaf of bread to eat, you wouldn't give the child a stone. Or if the child asks for a fish to eat, you wouldn't hand the child a snake! As imperfect a parent as you are, you know how to give good gifts to your children. Then how much more do you think your heavenly Parent God will do for the human children who want the gifts of the Holy Spirit in their lives? (*Matthew* 7:7-11; *Luke* 11:9-13)

"A good rule of thumb for living the life God will give you is this: treat other people the way you want them to treat you! (*Matthew* 7:12; *Luke* 6:31)

"There is a right way to live life to its fullest. You have to be deliberate in your search for it; you can't just live accidentally. There are a million ways to do something wrong, and only one way to do it perfectly right. The gate that leads to life is narrow, and the way is demanding. Few people find it. A lot of people walk that easy way that leads through the wide gate marked 'failure.' (*Matthew* 7:13-14; *Luke* 13:23-24)

'And just as there are many ways that will not lead to life, so there are many false advocates for those ways. Watch out for them. They come in sheep's clothing, but inwardly they are wolves with treacherous motives. Of course, you can check them by their actions and the results they bring in people's lives. You don't get grapes from a thornbush, or figs from a thistle. Good trees bear fruit, but bad trees don't. So you can tell good prophets from false prophets by the fruit they produce. The bad trees will eventually be cut down and thrown into the fire. Don't worry about them." (***Matthew*** 7:15-20; ***Luke*** 6:43-44) Then Luke adds one more verse explaining that "the good person produces good out of the good that is in his/her heart. The evil person produces bad out of an evil heart. The mouth just sounds off according to what is in the heart of the speaker.

"There are bad leaders, but there are poor followers too. The real prophet doesn't just talk. Neither does the real disciple. Not every one who says the words 'Lord, Lord' to me is going to enter the kingdom of heaven. Only the one who does the will of God will be a part of God's kingdom. There will come a judgment day when a good many people will say, 'Lord, we were right with You, even eating meals with You. You taught in our towns. More than that, we preached in Your name and did a great many wonderful acts of healing in Your name.' And I will have to say, 'I don't even recognize you; be gone, you evildoers.' (***Matthew*** 7:21-23; ***Luke*** 6:46; 13:26-27)

"I know that sounds hard," Jesus might have added, "but using my name is not an act of magic or a guarantee of God's approval. The thing that counts is the character a person builds in doing the will of God from pure motive and in a loving manner.

"A person who hears these words of mine and lives them is like a smart builder who built a house on solid rock foundation. Heavy rains, floods, high wind beat on that house but it never fell, because it had a solid foundation. But a person who hears my teachings and does not live according to them is like a foolish builder who lays the foundations for the house on sand. When the rains and floods come, and the winds beat on it, that house will fall. The crash will be spectacular." (***Matthew*** 7:24-27; ***Luke*** 6:47-49)

This is the way Jesus taught. All three gospel writers agree. And people were astonished because He didn't read it out of books and teach as the Scribes did; He talked from life experience. (***Matthew*** 7:28-29; ***Mark*** 1:21-22; ***Luke*** 4:31-32)

Success In Galilee

There is no way we can match the stories the writers tell and say for sure "this happened one week, this happened the next, and so on." Also no way to say what order His appearances at various towns and places ought to come exactly. But since we are using *Mark* as the editorial skeleton on which we are hanging the additional observations and reports of *Matthew* and *Luke*, we will follow Mark's order as closely as we can.

On one occasion Jesus went back into Capernaum, and rumor had it that He was in a certain house. Such a large crowd gathered that no one could go in or out the door. Jesus was talking with a group inside the house when four men came near the place carrying a paralyzed friend of theirs on a stretcher. When they found out they couldn't get near enough to Jesus to attract His attention, they worked their way up onto the roof, removed some tiles above Jesus' head, and lowered the paralyzed man through the opening.

When Jesus saw how much they believed He could help their sick friend, He said to the man on the stretcher, "My son, your sins are forgiven."

Inside that room were some Scribes, the official Jewish interpreters of the scriptures. They didn't say a word, but Jesus could sense what they were thinking. They were saying to themselves: "Why, nobody can forgive sins but God. This man is putting

Himself in God's place!''

So Jesus said to them, ''Why are you thinking what you are thinking? Would it have been easier for me to say 'Get up and walk' instead of saying, 'Your sins are forgiven?' Now I am going to prove to you that I have full authority to forgive sins. God wants this man to be forgiven, and God wants this man to be whole in every way.''

He turned back to the man and said ''Get up, pick up your bed and go home!''

At once the man sprang to his feet and picked up the stretcher. As the crowd shrank back in amazement from the doorway to give him room, He walked out in full view of the Scribes, making His way through the crowd. Everybody saw it, and everybody was saying, ''We've never seen anything like this before.'' (*Mark* 2:1-12; *Matthew* 9:1-8; *Luke* 5:17-26)

One of those who came for help one day in Capernaum was a Roman centurion, the commander of a hundred of the occupying troops. He had a slave who was also a close friend, and the slave was at the point of death. When he heard Jesus was in town again, the centurion asked friends of his among the Jewish religious community to beg Jesus to come to heal his slave. They put in a good word for the officer, saying ''He is a good man, a real friend of our people. In fact, he was the major contributor when we built our synagogue.''

So Jesus went with them, but when they got a short distance from his house, some other friends of the centurion met them with this message from him: ''Lord, You don't have to go to the trouble of coming to my house. I am not worthy to have a guest like You under my roof. That's why I didn't come to You in person. If You will just say the word, I know my servant will be healed. I am a man of authority. When I give a command, my soldiers or servants immediately do what I have ordered. So I am sure that You simply have to issue a command and the healing will be done."

Jesus was amazed. He turned and said to the crowd that was moving along with Him, "I tell you, nowhere in Israel have I found such faith as this man has. I tell you, too, that people will be coming from every other nation to sit down with Abraham, Isaac and Jacob in the kingdom of heaven, while many sons and daughters of Israel will be thrown out to spend their time crying over what they have missed."

The word to the centurion was a concise order: "Be it done for you as you have believed!" And the servant was healed. (*Matthew* 8:5-13; *Luke* 7:1-10)

So in or out of town, wherever Jesus went, the crowds were there with Him, and He used every opportunity to teach them.

One day as He was moving through the country and teaching as He went, a familiar question came from soneone who was confident about being one of a "chosen few" that God would accept. "Lord, will only a few be saved?"

"That will be up to every individual. The person who works at living God's way will find that narrow path, but many people will miss it. And when you have missed it, you may plead with God to let you in anyway:

"'Lord, open to us. We are Your own people. We have the record of Your teachings. We have been part of Your fellowship, and we have done a lot of good things in Your Name. We are automatically IN, aren't we?'

"'Sorry,' God will say, 'you don't become a part of the divine kingdom because of your ancestry. In fact, Abraham, Isaac, and Jacob and the great prophets of Israel will be sitting at the fellowship table with people from every other part of the gentile world, and you will be left out!''' (*Luke* 13:22-30)

He was in a city called Nain once, with the usual crowd following Him. It happened that they were near the city gate when they met a funeral procession. A widow, with many friends, was following the casket of her only son. Looking at her, Jesus was so moved with compassion for the grieving mother that He said, "Don't cry, please." And as He spoke to her He was moving beside the casket to lay His hand on it. The casket bearers stood still as Jesus called out, "Young man, I tell you, get up!" And the dead man sat up and began to talk.

"Here is your son! Don't cry anymore," Jesus told her.

People were struck with awe, then shouts of praise to God began to come from the crowd. "This must be a great prophet here with us," they said to each other. "Surely God has visited us."

So the reports about Him grew all the more through the whole country. (*Luke* 7:11-17)

Once when He was going through town Jesus saw a tax collector working in his office. In spite of the fact that he was a hated collector of taxes for the Roman rulers, Jesus saw something in this man Levi that made Him know that he would have great leadership qualities. He asked Levi to follow Him and be one of His disciples, and Levi (or Matthew) got up, left his business and went with Jesus.

Not long after that Jesus was in Levi's house having supper. Meanwhile the word of Levi's decision to follow Jesus had spread among the other tax collectors and people who were generally despised by Jewish religious leaders. These people wanted to come and see for themselves, so a group of them came into Levi's house where Jesus was eating with His disciples.

When the church officials saw Jesus eating in this company of tax collectors and irreligious people, they asked His disciples why He did it. Jesus overheard them asking the question and made this answer:

"The people who are well don't need a doctor, but those who are sick do. I didn't come to show the way to those who already know it, but to those who don't." (*Mark* 2:13-17; *Matthew* 9:9-13; *Luke* 5:27-32)

For the proud people who thought that they were more righteous than others, Jesus had another story.

"Two men went up to the temple to pray. One was a Pharisee, and the other was a tax collector for the Romans. This is the way the Pharisee prayed that day: 'Lord, I am so thankful that I am not like other people who do wicked things, people like this traitorous tax collector. You know that I fast twice a week, and I tithe every bit of my income.'

"But the tax collector, standing over in the corner of the court, wouldn't stand straight and look toward heaven. Bowed humbly, he beat his chest while he pleaded 'God, be merciful to me. I know I'm a sinner!'

"You know which man went back to his house accepted by God? The tax collector, not the Pharisee! Everyone who exalts himself will be humbled, but the one who humbles himself before God will be lifted up." (*Luke* 18:9-14)

"We ought always to pray and never lose hope," Jesus said. "There was a judge appointed by the Romans. He had no regard for God or for the rights of people. A certain widow in that city kept nagging him to decide a case in her favor. For a long while, he refused to give her any settlement, but she kept coming. Finally he said to himself, 'I'm tough, and I don't let my conscience bother me, but this woman is going to wear me out if I don't decide in her favor. So I'm going to do that just to get her off my back.'

"Listen, if a crooked judge will finally answer a persistent plea, how much more will God hear those who cry out in prayer day and night? I tell you, God will vindicate them even more surely. But will your faith in God's final answer hold out till the end?" (*Luke* 18:1-8)

The religious leaders also thought that Jesus did wrong in not telling His disciples to observe the "fast days" the times for going without food in order to concentrate on religious thought. John the Baptist's followers, as well as the Pharisees, observed certain days that they set aside for fasting.

"Why should My disciples take a day out to meditate about me when I am with them here? When the day comes that I am no longer with them in person, then they will have plenty of time to fast. After all, nobody sews a patch of cloth which has never been shrunk onto an old coat. If she does, when it is washed the new patch will shrink and tear away from the coat, and the hole will be worse than it ever was. And nobody puts unfermented grape juice into old wineskins. If he does, the new juice expands and the old dried skins are not able to expand, so they burst. The juice is spilled and the skins are ruined. No, if you are going to have new wine you have to put it into new wineskins, and if you are going to have a new life spirit you have to have new forms of expression and new rules of living. You can't force the new life back into the old religious rules." (*Mark* 2:18-22; *Matthew* 9:14-17; *Luke* 5:33-39) "Still, people will prefer the old ways, like old wine, because they are used to them," Luke adds.

Old sabbath rules must be called into question, Jesus had to decide again and again. One sabbath day Jesus and His disciples were walking by a wheat field. Some of His followers pulled off a few kernels of wheat to eat. Travelers were allowed to do that, but some Pharisees going along that road objected to their "working" on the sabbath day. Even "threshing" a few grains of wheat was listed as "work."

Jesus heard their objection and said, "Don't you remember reading about the time when David and his friends were hungry? He went into the shrine where Abiathar was the high priest, and he took the presentation loaves which only the priests are allowed to eat. All these sabbath rules," Jesus continued, "were made for people's benefit. Human Beings were not made to be slaves to the rules, but they are masters even of the sabbath." (*Mark* 2:23- 28; *Matthew* 12:1-8; *Luke* 6:1-5)

In Matthew's account, Jesus even cited another example of how priests in the great temple always break the sabbath work rules as they do all the labor connected with carrying out the sacrifices there. Why are they allowed to do it? Because the worship in temple sacrifices is more important than keeping the rules. Well, as prophets like Hosea said, human kindness is even more important than sacrifices in the temple. Human need takes precedence over all other rules or claims.

Then there was another sabbath when Jesus went into a synagogue where there was a man with a shriveled hand. Everyone was watching Jesus closely to see whether He would heal the man on the sabbath day. Then the Pharisees would have something more against Him.

"Stand up here in front of me," Jesus said to the man.

Then He said to the Pharisees, "Which is right on the sabbath day—to do good or to do harm? Is it better to save life or to kill?"

There was a dead slience. Jesus' anger mounted as He looked around at their callous faces. After a long moment, He answered His own question: "Which one of you if an animal of yours falls into a pit on the sabbath won't take hold of it and lift it out? Isn't a person more valuable than a sheep?" He said to the man, "Hold out your hand!" When he held it out, that hand was restored as healthy as the other one.

Immediately the Pharisees went out and began to plot with some of Herod's court, even though they would ordinarily have nothing to do with them. Now they were desperately looking for a way to get rid of Jesus. (*Mark* 3:1-6; *Matthew* 12:9-14; *Luke* 6:6-11)

As Jesus returned to the lakeside with His disciples, people from all over the country followed Him. From Galilee, Judea, Jerusalem, Idumea, from the country east of the Jordan River, and from the coastal cities of Tyre and Sidon they came because they had heard about what He was doing. The crowds pressed Jesus so closely that His disciples kept a boat ready for Him to step into. Everyone who was in pain was pushing forward trying to touch the One Who was healing so many. As soon as some recognized Who He was, they shouted,

"You are the Son of God."

But He asked them repeatedly not to stir up the crowd anymore." (*Mark* 3:7-12; *Matthew* 4:25, 12:15-21; *Luke* 6:17-19; 4:41)

Matthew, true to form, finds what he considers to be an Old Testament text which Jesus is fulfilling, *Isaiah* 42:1-4. It's about a specially chosen servant of God who will preach to gentiles in a gentle manner until justice is established everywhere and even the coastlands wait for His law.

A little later He went up a nearby mountainside, accompanied by a group He had selected from among His most faithful followers. There He chose a smaller group of twelve to be the inner circle of His disciples. To these He would give advanced training, so they would be able to preach His message and heal the sick. These were the twelve He appointed, a reminder of God's original covenant with the twelve tribes of Israel perhaps: Simon (whom Jesus called Peter),

Andrew (Simon's brother), James and John (the sons of Zebedee), Philip (another man from Bethsaida, hometown of Peter and Andrew), Bartholomew (probably the Nathanael mentioned in *John* 1:45), a friend of Philip's), Matthew (or Levi, the tax collector), Thomas, another James (son of Alphaeus, perhaps brother of Matthew since he also is noted as "son of Alphaeus"), Thaddaeus (called Judas, son of James, in Luke's list), another Simon (a member of the fiercely patriotic "zealot", or Cananaean party), and Judas Iscariot who would later betray Jesus to the authorities. (*Mark* 3:13-19; *Matthew* 10:1-4; *Luke* 6:12-16)

Of course, there were a good number of other men and women who wanted to be a part of the traveling school of disciples who accompanied this Master Teacher as Jesus now went into many villages and cities with His message of good news about the kingdom of God. *Luke* 8:1-3 names some of the women who not only traveled with the group, but who provided much of the provisions they needed. Mary, from a town called Magdala, who had some sort of unmentionable past, either morally or medically, was one who would be with Jesus' band to the end. Another was the wife of Chuza who was administrator of King Herod's business affairs. Her name was Joanna. A third was Susanna. And Luke says there were "many others." (The custom of the day would have prevented them from being "preachers" as the male disciples were, but nothing could stop them from telling what the friendship and guidance of Jesus was meaning to them. And probably their service spoke loudest of all.)

When He came back to town again such a crowd gathered that it was impossible even to eat a meal. Meanwhile, back in Nazareth, His family had been hearing of all this. So many of the Jewish religious leaders were saying that Jesus was acting very strangely that they set out to persuade Him to come back home with them.

Some scribes had come from headquarters in Jerusalem, and they were saying that Jesus was possessed by the Devil, and that Jesus could drive out devils only because He had joined with them. When Jesus heard this, He put this question to them:

"How can Satan be the one who drives out Satan? If a government is so split that one part is fighting against another part, then that government will fall. And if a home has fighting or division in it, it cannot last. It is stupid to think that the Devil is fighting against himself! ("By the way," Matthew's account adds here, "if I am kicking out demons by using the Devil's power, with whose power do your people kick them out? So judge yourselves. Then admit that if it is by the Spirit of God that I kick out demons, then the kingdom of God is here in my work.")

"Nobody can break into a house owned by a strong man and begin to steal his property without tying him up first. If the robber did that, he could ransack the house, of course. I am doing that to Satan's stronghold, and everyone who is not with me in this battle is against me. You can either help or hinder. But be very careful as you choose sides, because every sin can be forgiven except a refusal to listen to the Holy Spirit. If you won't heed God's Spirit, then what hope could there be for you ever? You may refuse to listen to a Human Being, and you can be forgiven for saying things against me, but when you say that the Holy Spirit within me is unclean, when you confuse the Spirit of God with the Devil, you are hopeless.

"No bad tree bears good fruit, does it? And no good tree produces bad fruit. You know a tree by its fruit. People are the same way. A good person brings good out of a good heart; the evil person brings evil out of an evil heart. Is that why you have so much trouble speaking good?

"On judgment day, everyone must account for every careless or hurtful word! (You do find out more about what a person really feels by words that "just slip out" than by the words she/he carefully plans to say.) (*Mark* 3:23-30; *Matthew* 12:25-37; *Luke* 11:17-23; 12:10, 6:43-45)

Soon afterward, His mother and His brothers came to town. They got to the edge of the large crowd outside the house and asked Him to come out to them. The message came through the crowd sitting around Him, "Your mother and brothers are outside asking for You."

Jesus' answer was this:

"Actually, who are my mother and my brothers?"

Then, as He looked around at the faces of some of His followers sitting around Him, He said "You see, these are my mother and my brothers and sisters too. Every person who lives as a good member of God's family is a brother and sister and mother to me." (*Mark* 3:31-35; *Matthew* 12:46-50; *Luke* 8:19-21)

A great deal of His teaching Jesus did by using stories. One time when He was by the edge of the lake, seated in a little boat with a huge crowd covering the ground right up to the water's edge, He told them this story, or parable:

"A farmer was out planting seed, and as he swung his arms scattering seed here and there some of the seed fell on the edge of the road and birds pecked it up immediately. Some of the seed fell on rocky soil. The plants came up quickly, but when the sun got hot, they were soon scorched and withered. The topsoil was so shallow that there were no deep roots. Some of the seed fell among thistles, and the thistles outgrew the grain and choked it out. But there was some seed which fell on good soil. It grew well and produced a good crop."

After the story Jesus added, "Everyone who has ears should use them."

Later, when they were by themselves, His close followers asked Him why He told that kind of story. He replied "When your heart is open to God, you can understand the truth of life that is hidden from others. Those who don't recognize the spirit of the kingdom of God are fulfilling the words Isaiah spoke of them:

"'They have eyes to see but cannot perceive, and ears to hear but cannot understand; for if they did they would turn to God and be forgiven.'"

"So I hope you really understand this story I told. If you don't get the point of this one you won't understand all the other stories I tell either. The farmer planting the seed is like a person telling the message of the kingdom of God. Like the seed by the roadside some hear it but immediately other thoughts and interests take it out of their minds. The seed scattered on rocky soil represents those people who hear the message and accept it with enthusiasm at first. But they haven't thought it through deeply enough and they don't hold to the faith when trouble or persecution comes. And the seed among the thistles? Those are the people who hear the message, but worries and the appeal of money and material possessions and all sorts of ambitions gradually creep in and choke out their spiritual life. But the seed planted in good soil represents those who hear the message and believe it. They go to work for God and produce a good crop, spreading the kingdom of God idea to many others." (*Mark* 4:1- 20; *Matthew* 13:1-23; *Luke* 8:4-15)

He followed that up be adding:

"What is a lamp for? To put under a basket or under a bed? Or do you put it on a stand so that it can light the room? A lot of things seem mysterious or hidden now but someday they will be understood. What you think are secrets of the universe will one day be common knowledge. So use your brains to think.

"And be very careful to get this one point about life: the way you judge other people will decide what you are going to get from life yourself. The person who learns how to live really has something, and that person will keep getting more and more from life. But the person who never learns how to live God's way has nothing, and in the long run will lose out completely." (*Mark* 4:21-25; *Matthew* 13:12; *Luke* 8:16-18)

Farm stories were good ones to get His point across apparently. In talking about how the kingdom of God comes, Jesus said, "It is like a farmer planting wheat. The farmer goes about the regular business day after day and all the time the seeds are sprouting and the plants are growing. Nobody has any idea how it happens. The farmer doesn't produce the crop. The earth does. First, the stalk, then the grain develops until finally the kernels of wheat are full grown. Just as soon as it is ripe, the workers get into the field with their sickles because the time for harvesting has come." (*Mark* 4:26-29)

Here's another one in *Matthew* 13:24-30.

The kingdom of heaven can be compared to a farmer planting good seed in the field, but an enemy comes at night and sows weed seeds among the wheat seeds. When the crop begins to grow, the weeds are thick in the field with the wheat. "What's this?" the farm helpers ask the farm owner, "How come these weeds are growing in the wheat field? Didn't you plant good seed?"

"I'm afraid somebody has done this in an attempt to ruin our crop," the farmer answered.

"Well," they said, "do you want us to get out there and pull out all the weeds we can?"

"No," he said, "you might pull up some wheat along with the weeds and we will lose part of our crop. Let it all grow together. When harvest time comes I'll have the reapers take all the weeds first and burn them, then the wheat we can put into the barn."

"If you really want to think about how the kingdom of God grows," Jesus said at another time, "consider a mustard seed. It is about the smallest of all the various seeds that are planted in the ground. But when it comes up, it produces one of the largest bushes, big enough for birds to nest in its branches." (*Mark* 4:30-32; *Matthew* 13:31-32; *Luke* 13:18-19)

"Or look at it this way. The kingdom of heaven is like yeast which a cook takes and mixes into a large batch, about eight gallons, of meal, and that little yeast makes the whole dough rise." (*Matthew* 13:33; *Luke* 13:20-21)

Sometimes in private He went into greater detail about a good many things with His disciples, but ordinarily in His speaking to larger groups He used simple stories like these. Once, in private, *Matthew* adds: "His disciples asked Him to explain the meaning of the story about the weeds in the wheat field. Jesus' answer went like this:

"'"The farmer sowing the good seed is like the Son of Man; the field is the world; the good seeds are like the good people who are part of the kingdom of God, and the weeds are like people who oppose God's rule. The enemy who sows the weeds is the devil; the harvest represents the close of this age; and the angels are the reapers. The weeds are gathered and burned, just as the wicked people and all causes of sin will be rooted out and cast aside to be destroyed at the time of judgment. Too late they will grind their teeth in misery, but the good-seed people will be gathered into the kingdom of God. Now do you get it?"'"

There were non-farm stories too. So important is

the kingdom-of-heaven life that being a part of it should be the Number One priority for every person. Like a man finding a buried treasure. He sells everything he owns in order to get enough money to buy that field so the treasure will be his. Or like a jewel merchant who sees one pearl that is clearly superior to all others. He, too, sells everything he has in order to get the price of that pearl.

The good seed and weeds story could be told the same way for fisherfolk. Instead of a field and seeds, you have the sea and fish. A net draws in both good and trash fish, just as the harvesters cut both weeds and wheat. Again the bad is separated from the good at judgment time, and the bad ones end up gnashing teeth once more. The kingdom of God gives you the option.

"If you have understood all this," Jesus told them, "you will see that every person who is trained to sort out the things that are consistent with the kingdom of heaven from those that are not will be like a householder who has a useful mixture of traditional values and new ideas." (*Matthew* 13:36-52)

Days of Decision

''If we get there early,'' some of the guests who had been invited to a wedding banquet were saying among themselves, ''we can get the best seats near the head table.'' Of course, Jesus did not miss the opportunity to make a suggestion about the wisdom of humility.

''You might be embarrassed if somebody more important has also been invited. The host may have to ask you to give up your place to the more prominent guest and you will have to take a lower seat. It would be better to go sit in the seat at the end of the table. Then when the host sees you there and says 'My friend, come up here to a better place near me,' everyone will notice the honor the host is giving you.

''It's true in life that the person who tries to exalt himself or herself will end up being humbled, but the person who doesn't grasp for honor will be recognized for his or her own worth.''

Jesus also had a word for people who have money enough to put on extravagant parties.

''When you give a banquet, try this sometime. Instead of inviting your family or your rich neighbors, because you know they will repay you by inviting you to their next dinner, invite some poor people, some crippled and blind people who can never repay you. Your reward will come then at the time when the truly just people are resurrected into eternal life.'' (*Luke* 14:7-14)

''Amen,'' one of His hearers added enthusiastically. ''A person is really blessed to end up eating at God's banquet table.''

''Yes, but think about this,'' Jesus replied. ''One time a man was giving a big banquet. A lot of people were invited, but when the servants went out to tell them that the dinner was finally ready none of them came. Thinking there must be some mistake, the man sent his servants back to them. ''Tell them that the meat is all prepared and everything is ready now.''

But everyone had an excuse. One of them said ''I just bought a field and I have to go and check it out. Sorry, I just can't make it to the banquet.'' Another said ''I got this good deal on five yoke of oxen, and I will just have to go and try them out.'' A third one pulled the old Adam trick, ''If it wasn't for my new wife I could make it.''

The servants came back to the host and told him that none of the invited guests were going to show up.

''In that case I have another plan,'' the host said angrily. ''Go out all over town and invite all the poor and crippled and blind people you can find. They won't make excuses.''

When the servants returned, there still were not enough people to fill the house completely, so the host sent them out again: ''Bring everybody you see; we are going to have a full house at this banquet, and not one of the guests I originally invited will get a taste of these treats.'' (*Luke* 14:15-24; *Matthew* 22:1-10)

That story was pointed enough for those who were listening to Jesus as people who were sure that God's banquet would be prepared for their nation only. But *Luke* follows it up with an account of Jesus' saying that total costly commitment is necessary if anyone is going to be a part of His group at the awards dinner.

''To be a disciple of mine, a person has to make the kingdom of God the Number One Priority, ahead of family or even life itself. In fact, you have to be willing every day to be crucified with me. So consider the cost of this discipleship very carefully.

"If one of you wants to build a watchtower in your vineyard, don't you first sit down and estimate the cost so that you will be sure you have enough money to complete the job? If you don't you may have a part of a tower sitting there for everyone to see and make jokes about. You'll feel foolish when they say 'He started to build it and wasn't able to finish it.'

"Or think about a king planning on engaging another king in war. If he has only ten thousand men to throw up against twenty thousand the other king has, shouldn't he think through how he is going to fight? And if he decides the odds are too much against him, doesn't he send an envoy before the fighting starts to ask the terms of peace? So I am telling you to count the cost before you plan to be a disciple of mine." (*Luke* 14:7-32)

"The kingdom of God I came to announce brings the fire of judgment on the world. I have to go through this baptism of hurt and sorrow until my task is accomplished! Don't think that there won't be any hardship or struggle in following my Way. No, there will be plenty of division and animosity caused. Even in the same household, a family will be divided one against another when some accept me and others do not." (*Luke* 12:49-53)

Late one afternoon Jesus suggested to His disciples that they go across the lake because it was the only way they could get around the crowds on the shore. Before they left, one of the Jewish scribes came up and said "Teacher, I will follow You wherever You go."

"Foxes have their dens, and birds of the air have their nests, but I don't even have a place now to lay down to sleep," Jesus came back as a way of warning

"It won't be as easy as you think; better think through your decision very carefully." Did he thoroughly understand that Jesus' way would mean an end to all the legalism to which the scribe presently devoted his life?

But Jesus' answer was not always the same. It depended on the person. When another would-be follower said "I will come, but first let me go and take care of my father; when he is dead I will be free to follow you." Jesus said, "Leave that to others. You come now and follow me. Don't put it off." (*Matthew* 8:18-22; *Luke* 9:57-60)

Finally they pushed off in the boats. Out on the lake one of those sudden storms for which the Sea of Galilee is famous swept over them, driving waves into the boats. The men woke Him up with their shouts:

"Master, how can You sleep? We're about to drown."

He woke up and simply said to the lake, "Stop it. Be calm!"

The wind died immediately and everything was calm.

Then He turned and spoke to the men who were so amazed that they didn't know what to do.

"Why were you so scared? What happened to your faith?"

When they were finally able to speak, they kept saying to themselves, "Who in the world can He be? Even the wind and the lake do what He tells them."

When they arrived on the other side of the lake, they were in the country of the Gerasenes. Just as Jesus got out of the boat, an insane man came running toward Him. This man lived among the tombs. He had such tremendous strength that ropes and chains could not hold him. Several times people had tried to tie him up, but he had always broken loose and run away. At night they could hear him screaming among the tombs where he gashed his legs and arms with sharp stones. Now this wild man came charging toward Jesus, but when he got near Him he knelt down, yelling at the top of his voice, "What are You going to do with me, You Son of God? Don't torture me, for God's sake!"

Jesus looked at him calmly, then sharply commanded, "Get out of this man, you evil spirit!"

Then He spoke to the man. "What is your name?"

"They call me Legion," he replied, "because there are many parts to me. Please, please, don't send us out of the country."

There was a herd of about 2,000 pigs grazing nearby on this gentile hillside. All of a sudden the whole herd began to stampede over the cliff and into the lake where they drowned. When the swineherders ran into the city to tell about it, they reported that Jesus had sent the evil spirits out of the man called Legion into the herd of pigs. They believed that evil spirits had to have bodies to live somewhere. And many of the people rushed out of town to see what had happened. As they came near to where Jesus was camped, they saw the man who had been so violently insane and they couldn't believe their eyes. The wild man was sitting there fully dressed and in his right mind.

Now they were frightened, because they knew that something great and mysterious had taken place. They begged Jesus to leave their section of the country, and He did. As He was getting back into the boat, the man who had been insane kept saying that he wanted to go with Him, but Jesus would not allow him to go.

"Go home to your people," Jesus told him, "and tell everybody what God has done for you!"

That's exactly what the man did. He went through the whole region of the "Ten Towns" and spread the story of what Jesus had done for him, and people were amazed.

So back across the lake they went, and as usual a big crowd gathered around Him. One of the men who came this time was a synagogue president named Jairus. He knelt before Jesus, begging for help.

"My little daughter is dying," he said. "If You will just come and lay Your hands on her, I know she will live and get well."

Followed by the large crowd which was pressing all around Him, Jesus hurried home with Jairus. In that crowd was a woman who had been bleeding internally for twelve years. She had gone to every doctor in the country and had spent all her money trying to get healed, but she was only getting worse. Slipping through the crowd, this woman came up behind Jesus. She really believed that if she could just touch His clothes she would be healed. And she was! The moment she touched His cloak she knew that she was cured of her trouble. At that moment Jesus stopped. He had sensed that the healing had occurred.

"Who touched my clothes?" He asked the jostling crowd. His disciples were amazed.

"Why, people are crowding all around You. Everybody is pushing against You." But He stood still, looking at their faces to see if He could spot the person. Now, frightened and trembling all over, the woman threw herself on the ground before Him and began to pour out her story.

"Daughter, your faith has healed you," Jesus said kindly. "You can go home without any fear and be free from your trouble."

Just then messengers from the synagogue president's house came rushing up.

"Your little daughter has died. There won't be any need for the Master to come now."

When Jesus heard this, He said to Jairus, "Don't give up hope. Go on trusting God." Then He turned to the crowd and asked that no one follow Him on to the house except Peter, James and John. When they got to the president's house, they found a crowd of people weeping and wailing. Inside the house Jesus asked a loud question, "Why are you folks making such a racket? This child is not dead; she is just unconscious!"

Some of them laughed scornfully, but they left the house as Jesus moved them out. Then, taking only the father and mother and His three disciples with Him, He went into the room where the twelve-year-old was lying. Gently, He took the little girl's hand in His and said to her, "Wake up, honey!" Immediately, the girl opened her eyes and got up. Her parents were overcome with joy, but Jesus asked that they did not talk around about what had happened, then thoughtfully suggested that they might bring the daughter something to eat. (*Mark* 5:21-43; *Matthew* 9:18-26; *Luke* 8:40-56)

Then there was the time Jesus and His disciples came to His hometown of Nazareth. *Mark* tells that story in 6:1-6. *Matthew* puts it in chapter 13:53-58. Essentially it is the same sad story *Luke* ties in to Jesus' announcement of His call to be God's anointed messenger (see page 18 of this copy).

After the Nazareth visit, He continued on to neighboring towns, teaching as He went. It was at this time of His ministry that He began to send the disciples out two by two to preach and to heal. Luke says there once were seventy of them who went as a sort of preparation team in the places He Himself planned to visit later. He advised them to take nothing with them as they went, except one change of clothes. They didn't even take food or money in their pockets. "You deserve the food you get," Jesus told them, "but don't take any pay. You received this good news without paying for it; give it to others the same way.

Perhaps others will follow your example and join you. Pray that they will because the harvest is so plentiful, and the laborers are so few!''

He told them, ''When you are staying in a town, don't move around from house to house; but make your headquarters in one place as long as you stay there. If you come to a town where people will not welcome you and won't listen to what you have to say, just leave and go on down the road.''

So they left and began to preach that people should change their way of living. And they, too, were able to heal many sick people. (*Mark* 6:6-13; *Matthew* 9:35, 10:1, 9-11, 14; *Luke* 2:1-6; also 10:1-16)

In Luke's story, when the seventy got back they were bursting with enthusiasm. ''Lord,'' they exclaimed, ''even the evil spirits in people could be controlled by us when we used Your name!''

''Yes, I know,'' He said, ''but remember that Satan fell from heaven because of pride. I have given you the authority to put down evil and to cure illness, and as long as you keep that faith nothing will hurt you. But this new power is not what you should be rejoicing about; just be glad always that your names are included in the list of those who have found heaven!'' (*Luke* 10:17-20)

Jesus shared His own sense of victory with them by praying ''I thank You, my God, Creator of all heaven and earth and us, that You have hidden those deep truths and joys from the learned and clever people and yet revealed them to simple people who see life with the eyes of children! I know now that I've got it. I know You, and You have given me this life relationship with You which I can share with others. From now on they can see You in me!''

Then, turning to His disciples, He said ''What a privilege it is for Human Beings to know what you now know! For centuries prophets and kings wanted to understand this revelation of God but never got to see or hear it as you have." (*Luke* 10:21-24; *Matthew* 11:25-27; 13:16-17)

As word of Jesus spread all over the country, Herod the king had heard the news too. Many people were saying that Jesus was really John the Baptist come back to life. Others said He was Elijah, and still others were guessing that He was one of the other prophets who had come back. When Herod heard the talk, He also believed that it must be John whom he had beheaded a short time before. His conscience was still tender about what he had done.

Herod had sent his men to take John and shut him up in prison because John had condemned Herod for taking his brother Philip's wife, Herodias. John had publicly asserted that the marriage was not legal. Herodias hated John and would have had him killed instead of jailed, but she couldn't persuade Herod to do it because the king still had a deep respect for John. Although John spoke plainly to him and disturbed him, Herod somehow still enjoyed hearing John and realized in his heart that John was right.

One night Herodias got her opportunity. The king gave a big birhday party to which he invited the leading people from his court, his army commanders and the high society people from all over Galilee. For part of the entertainment, Herodias' daughter thrilled the group with her exotic dance. Herod got so carried away with her performance that he said "Ask me anything you like and I will give it to you!" He even added an oath that he would give her whatever she wanted, up to half the kingdom!

The dancing daughter went out and asked her mother, "What shall I ask for?"

And her mother seized the opportunity. "Ask for the head of John the Baptist."

The girl went right back in to the king. "I want you

to give me right now the head of John the Baptist on a platter."

Herod was shocked, but he had sworn an oath in the presence of his guests, and he wouldn't go back on it. (Shades of some of the Old Testament stories!) He sent one of the palace guards to the prison with orders to bring back John's head. The executioner moved into John's prison cell, cut off John's head, and sent it on a platter back to the girl who handed it to her mother.

When John's disciples heard what had happened, they hurried to the prison and asked for the body. They took it away and buried it in a tomb, and then they found Jesus and told Him what had happened. (***Mark*** 6:14-29; ***Matthew*** 14:1-12; ***Luke*** 9:7-9)

Meanwhile His own disciples had returned from their preaching tour to make their reports to Him of what they had done since He sent them out.

"Let's go someplace where we can be alone for a while," Jesus suggested, since people were crowding around them so much where they were that they could hardly take time for meals and couldn't get any rest.

So they got in their boats and went off to be by themselves. But people saw them go, and crowds of them followed along the shore. When the boats put in to land, Jesus saw a bigger crowd than ever waiting. He felt sorry for them because they were looking so desperately for help of one kind or another. They seemed like a big flock of sheep without a shepherd. So as soon as they landed He began to speak to them once more. All day He taught and, when it was getting late in the afternoon, His disciples began to say "We're a long way from any town here. Night is coming and these folks haven't had anything to eat all day. Maybe we should break up this meeting so everybody can get out somewhere and find something to eat at the nearest farms and settlements."

But Jesus answered, "Why don't you give them something to eat?"

"What? It would take a lot of money to buy bread for all this outfit. Do you want us to do that?"

"Well, let's see," Jesus said. "How much bread do you have here already? Check on that first."

After a little bit, they reported, "We have five little loaves of bread and two fish."

"That's plenty," Jesus decided. "Bring them to me." Then He began to organize the large mass of people into smaller groups of fifty to a hundred each and told them to sit down together on the grass. That done, He took the five loaves and two fish and, after praying, told the disciples to start distributing the food. The stories don't say how the bread and fish were divided, but the supply held out somehow until everyone was fed. Even after all had had their fill, there were still twelve baskets full left over. A ministerial estimate of the crowd was put at "five thousand men, plus women and children." (*Mark* 6:30-44; *Matthew* 14:13-21; *Luke* 9:10-17)

After everything was cleaned up, Jesus sent His disciples down to the boat to go back across the lake to Bethsaida while He stayed behind to send the people home. As soon as they were all gone away, He went farther up the mountainside to pray by Himself. The wind He felt on His face was directly against the boat which was already out in the middle of the lake. The disciples were straining at the oars, trying to make headway against it. All that night they had to keep the boat headed into the wind to keep it from turning over, and in the very early hours of the dawn Jesus saw them still out there and went walking toward them on the lake. When they saw Him they thought He was a ghost and were scared almost to death.

"Don't be afraid," He called out, "everything is all

right; it is I myself."

Here *Matthew* adds a paragraph that was dearly loved among Christians in the next few generations who used it for a text in telling each other that they would be able to weather any storm of persecution or misfortune as long as they kept their attention on Jesus instead of the storm. They pointed to Peter who learned the lesson as this story tells it:

"And Peter answered Jesus, 'Lord, if it is You, permit me to come to You on the water.'"

Jesus said "All right, come to me." So Peter actually stepped out of the boat and started walking across the water toward Jesus. Then, suddenly, he lost his nerve. He saw the wind whipping up the waves and he froze with fear. Beginning to sink, he cried out, "Lord, save me!" Jesus simply reached out His hand and caught hold of Peter saying, "You almost had it made; why did you doubt? Your faith wasn't quite strong enough."

Then Jesus got into the boat with them and the wind stopped blowing. They were all utterly astounded. "Truly, You are the Son of God!" one of them said, and they all nodded agreement.

Mark says that after Jesus got in the boat the disciples were so badly shaken that their eyes were still not opened to Who He really was, even though they had just witnessed the feeding of the five thousand and now this miracle.

With the storm calmed down, they were able to cross over to the other side of the lake and land at Genesaret. They had barely tied up the boat there before people recognized Jesus, and they ran all over the countryside telling the news, so that people began bringing their sick ones to see Him. Everywhere He went, whether in the towns or out in the open country, they laid their sick people right down in the middle of the road and begged just to be able to touch the hem of His cloak. And so great was His power and their faith in Him that all who touched Him were healed.

Once again He encounters Pharisees and their scribes who had come from the Jerusalem headquarters. Watching for any and every thing they could find to criticize, they observed that His disciples did not go through the traditional Jewish ceremony of washing their hands before they ate their meals. The religious Jew is not supposed to eat any time until the hands have been washed in a particular way, and they will not eat anything bought in a market without first "sprinkling" it according to a traditional rule. There are a good many other little ceremonies connected with the washing of eating utensils which devout Jews are supposed to observe. That's why the Pharisees and scribes asked Jesus:

"Why don't Your disciples keep the religious rules about eating?"

Jesus answered quickly, "You big talkers! Isaiah described you exactly when he said 'These people talk constantly about honoring Me, but they do not really worship Me in their hearts. They are busy teaching a bunch of man-made ideas as if they were My laws.'

"You are so busy trying to observe every little religious rule that you have overlooked the real intentions of God." Then He went on, "It's a strange thing how you sometimes change God's commandments to suit yourselves. Moses said 'Honor your father and your mother.' He also said 'He who speaks ill of his father and his mother should die.' But you say that if a man simply announces to his father and mother that he is giving to God whatever duty he owed to them that he doesn't have to lift a finger from then on to help his parents. So you make over the Word of God to suit your own tradition and practice. And this is just the way it is with so much that you do."

Then He addressed the whole crowd again:

"Now hear this, all of you, and don't miss the point. There is nothing outside a person that can go into the person to make him or her bad. It is the things that come out that show a person up for what he or she is."

Later on, when they were indoors away from the crowd, His disciples wondered about that statement He had made.

"Well, are you as dense as everybody else?" Jesus said. "Can't you see that physical things which go into a person's body don't affect the character? They go into the stomach, not the heart. Finally, they pass out of the body altogether. But it is what is inside a person that makes the difference. It is from a person's mind that evil thoughts come—evil desires, stealing, murder, adultery, greed, wickedness, deceit, passion, envy, slander, pride, foolishness! All these come from inside and make a person unclean." (***Mark*** 6:45, 7:23; ***Matthew*** 14:22, 15:20)

Matthew slips in a note that Jesus' disciples felt they had to point out the obvious after His exchange with the Pharisees. "Do you know that the Pharisees were offended at what You said?" Jesus turned that away by saying "Every plant which God has not planted will be rooted up in the end. So let them alone; they are blind guides. And if the blind leads the blind, both of them will fall into a ditch." ***Luke*** 6:39 remembers this same statement from Jesus.

(Since our culture is so different, it would be easy for us to miss the enormous break with religious tradition and much scripture which Jesus is making here. We thank *Matthew* for making sure it isn't overlooked by the reader. Jesus throws out all the food laws of the Old Testament. Religion is a matter of the heart, not of hygiene. If much of religion isn't a matter of trying to please God by keeping rules and regulations, then most of what the Pharisees were teaching and doing was worthless. More than that, it was dangerous, for it misled the people who followed them, like blind leading the blind! When the disciples said that the Pharisees were "offended" by what Jesus said, they were masters of understatement.)

For the first time now, Jesus left Galilee and went off to the neighborhood of Tyre on the Mediterranean coast. When He got to town, He went to one particular house hoping that no one would know where He was. But He had the same experience here as everywhere else. Just as soon as He arrived, one woman came up and knelt before Him. This Greek woman, not one of the Jews, had a daughter with some kind of mental illness, and she begged Jesus to drive "the evil spirits" out of her daughter.

Then Jesus said what His disciples and any other staunch Jews there were probably thinking.

"You must let God's special children eat all they want first. It is not right, you know, to take food from in front of the children and throw it to the dogs."

But the woman replied quickly, "Yes, I know, Master, but the dogs under the table do get to eat what the children leave."

"If you can come back with an answer like that," Jesus said to her, "you can go home and know that the evil spirit has gone out of your daughter."

The woman hurried home and found the child perfectly well, lying quietly on her own bed. (*Mark* 7:24-30; *Matthew* 15:21-28)

On His way back from Tyre toward the lake of Galilee, Jesus passed through Sidon and finally across the territory of the Ten Towns. Once during this journey they brought to Him a man who was deaf and unable to speak so that anyone could understand him, and they begged Jesus to put His hands on this man. Jesus led the man away from the crowd, off to one side. He stuck His fingers into the man's ear, and then He took some of His own saliva and touched it to the tip of the man's tongue. (The man certainly knew that Jesus was focusing His attention upon his ears and mouth.) After He had done that, Jesus looked toward heaven, breathed a big sigh, and then gave the command: "Open!"

Immediately the man could hear and speak quite plainly. Right away Jesus asked everyone not to tell about this, but they couldn't keep it quiet. They discussed it all over that part of the country, and everywhere you could hear the amazed comment,

"Isn't He terrific! He even makes the deaf hear and the dumb speak. He does everything well." (*Mark* 7:31- 37; *Matthew* 15:29-31)

Again a large crowd gathered without adequate provisions for themselves. Jesus called His disciples to one side and said,

"I feel awfully sorry for this crowd. They have been out here listening to me for three days, and there is nothing left to eat. Some of them have come from such a great distance that I can't send them home without anything to eat; they might collapse on the way."

"Well, where are we going to get food out here in this deserted place?" they asked. "How many loaves of bread do you have left?" Jesus inquired.

"Seven," they answered.

Then Jesus announced that everyone should be seated on the ground, and He took the seven loaves into His hands. As He prayed a prayer of thanksgiving, He broke the bread, giving the pieces to the disciples to distribute to the people. They also had a few fish, so Jesus did the same thing with them. Everybody ate and was satisfied, and after the meal was over they gathered up seven baskets full of pieces.

There were about four thousand people in that

crowd that Jesus sent home while He and His disciples went to get in their boats to go down the lake to the district of Dalmanutha. (*Mark* 8:1-10; *Matthew* 15:32-39)

Here He had another argument with the Pharisees who kept saying that they wanted to see a "sign from heaven."

"When you see a cloud rising in the west," Jesus answered them and the crowd which was listening, "you may say to each other 'A shower is coming.' And it does. When you feel the south wind blowing, you say 'There's scorching heat on the way.' Sure enough, it comes. You all know how to interpret the natural signs of the earth and sky. Why can't you interpret the signs of what is happening in our life together? You don't need any more sign than the sign of the prophet Jonah." And Jonah's only "sign" to Ninevah was himself and his message of repentance which meets God's forgiving love. (*Mark* 8:11-13; *Matthew* 16:1-4, also 12:38-39; *Luke* 11:16, 29, 12:54-56)

"On judgment day, when this generation is being considered, one of those who condemn it will be the queen of Sheba who made that long trip from her country just to hear the wisdom of King Solomon. Well, something greater than Solomon's wisdom is being said here. And the people of Ninevah who repented because of the preaching of Jonah will also condemn this generation for not hearing a greater message you are hearing." (*Matthew* 12:41- 42; *Luke* 11:31-32)

"The kingdom of God is not coming with 'signs' and unusual events to be observed. It won't be something that people can point to and say 'There it is!' The kingdom of God is in you." (*Luke* 17:20-21)

"Of course, if we aren't careful, the victory over an evil spirit is only temporary. The bad ones never give up. Always remember the man who kicked out an unclean spirit but did not bring a good one to take its place. The evil spirit wandered around looking for a place to live, but found none so it came back to its old home. The man's life was all swept out and clean, but it was empty. So the bad spirit hurried and got seven more bad ones, all worse than itself. They all moved in and the last state of the man was worse than the first.

"All cleaned up legally, this generation will end up that way." (*Matthew* 12:43-45; *Luke* 11:24-26)

So He left them, got in the boat again to go back across the lake. But this time it was His own disciples who had forgotten to bring any food, and there was only one small loaf in the boat with them.

Jesus was still thinking about that conversation about "signs," and the first thing He said to His friends was "You are going to have to keep your eyes open! You are going to have to be on your guard against the 'yeast' of the Pharisees and against the 'yeast' of Herod."

The disciples had their minds on bread, and they thought He was getting after them for not bringing any along on this trip. At least that is what they were saying to each other when Jesus interrupted to say, "Why all this talk about no bread along? Don't you understand even yet what I am trying to say? Surely you are not like the people who 'have eyes and do not see and have ears but do not hear.' Have you forgotten already the time I broke five loaves of bread for five thousand people? How many basketsfull of pieces did you pick up after it was over?"

"Twelve," they answered.

"And when there were only seven loaves to feed the four thousand, how many pieces did you pick up?"

"Seven," they replied.

"And still you don't get the meaning of all that?"

He asked. We were dealing with bread then, but when I tell you to beware of the yeast of the Pharisees I am not talking about bread to eat. I am saying that the same kind of hypocrisy (see *Luke* 12:1) that makes a show of their religion could work its way into your life." (*Mark* 8:14-21; *Matthew* 16:5-12)

When they arrived at Peter's hometown of Bethsaida, a blind man was brought to Jesus in the hope that He could heal him. Jesus took the blind man by the hand and led him out of the village. He wet His fingers with saliva and touched the man's eyes. Then He laid His hands on his head and asked,

"Can you see anything at all?"

The man looked around and said "I can see people, but I can't make them out distinctly. They look like trees walking around."

So Jesus touched his eyes once more, and the man's sight came into focus. He could see everything sharply and clearly. "Now, go home to your own house," Jesus told him. "Don't go through the village and tell everyone about this." (*Mark* 8:22-26)

The word came through some Pharisees that King Herod was out to kill Him. "Better get out of here right away," they advised.

"You can go and tell that fox that I am doing my work of healing and teaching for a few more days here," Jesus answered. "After that I will be moving on to Jerusalem because it wouldn't be right for a prophet to die anywhere else." (*Luke* 13:31-33)

Jesus' next trip with His disciples was to the villages of Caesaria Philippi. On the way, He asked the disciples, "Who are people saying that I am?"

"Some say You are John the Baptist," they answered, "but others say that You are Elijah or one of the old prophets come back to life."

"But what about you. . .who do you say that I am?" Jesus asked them directly.

And Peter answered as the idea dawned in his mind, "You are the Messiah our people have always longed for, the Son of the living God!"

Again here, *Matthew* adds to the brief conversation.

"Simon, you are blessed indeed," Jesus said. "That insight had to come from God, and on that insight you will stand solid as a rock. That's why I call you Peter ("Petros" was the name in Greek, close to "petra", the word for "rock.") and on this rock I will build my Church. And all the powers of death will not be able to defeat this fellowship. I will give you who know this truth the keys to the kingdom of heaven. The decisions you will make will affect people here on earth forever.

"Now that you know I am the Christ (Messiah), let's keep it a secret for a while."

From that time on, Jesus began to tell them that He would have to go through a lot of suffering, and that He would be completely rejected by their religious leaders; one day they would kill Him, but that He would rise from the dead in three days.

Peter reacted so much to that kind of talk that he drew Jesus aside and told Him not to talk like that. But Jesus turned back to face His disciples so that all could hear His answer to Peter.

"Get out of my way, Satan! You're not looking at things from God's point of view now, Peter, but from a human point of view!" (*Mark* 8:27-33; *Matthew* 16:13- 23; *Luke* 9:18-22)

It was time that He speak plainly about the possible consequences of their continuing to be disciples and advocates of His. And He made it very plain more than once.

"If anybody wants to come along with me, that person is going to have to be willing to sacrifice self completely. The one who tries to save his or her own life will lose it. But the one who is willing to give up his/her life for my sake and for the Gospel will really save it. What good is it going to do anyway if a person gains the whole world and has to give up one's soul in the process of doing it? Once a person has lost his or her own soul, how much can be offered to buy it back?

"I tell you right now that if anybody is ashamed of me and my words, and won't stand up for me in this unbelieving world, then I will be ashamed of that person when we meet on the day this world is judged. (*Mark* 8:34-38; *Matthew* 16:24-27; *Luke* 9:23-26)

"A student is not ranked above the teacher, nor a slave above the master. The disciple is trying to be like the teacher, and the servant is trying to imitate the master. So, just think, if they call the master of a household a devil, how much worse will they malign the members of the household? (*Matthew* 10:24)

"Relax. Everything will be shown up for what it is finally. What is hidden will be uncovered, and everything that is whispered in private will be announced in public. Truth will out.

"Don't be afraid of people who can only kill your body but not your soul, but regard only the One Who can destroy both body and soul like trash in the valley of Henna. Don't worry; not even a sparrow which sells for half a penny in the market can light on the ground without God's knowing it. Aren't you worth a lot more than sparrows? In fact, the very hairs on your head are numbered in the sight of God Who cares infinitely for each one of you.

"But you can't have it both ways. Stand up for me and I will assure God that you are on Our side. If you won't stand up for me here, I cannot acknowledge you as my followers there.

"You mustn't think that I have come to preach 'peace at any price.' I know that my message will cause division and fighting, and the worst part of it is that people of the same household will become enemies because of me—a son against a father, daughter against a mother, daughter-in-law against mother-in-law. But it has to be. Loyalty to me and my kingdom must come first, even of loyalty and love for intimate family members. And if a person isn't willing to carry the crossbeam (as a condemned man going to a Roman crucifixion), then that person cannot be my disciple!'' (*Matthew* 10:26-39; *Luke* 12:2-9; 14:26-27; 17:33)

Then He added, ''Believe me, some of you who are standing right here now will still be alive to see the kingdom of God come in its power!'' (*Mark* 9:1; *Matthew* 16:28; *Luke* 9:27)

Testing and Training

About a week later Jesus took Peter, James and John and He went high on a hillside to be away from the crowd. Right before their very eyes His whole appearance began to change. His clothes became dazzling white, and they saw Elijah and Moses standing there having a conversation with Jesus. We are not told how the disciples recognized the ancient ones, but Peter felt that something ought to be said,

"Master, this is tremendous! Shall we make three little monuments here—one for you, one for Moses, and one for Elijah?"

Actually, he was so frightened he didn't know what he was saying. Then a cloud came over them all, and out of the cloud the three disciples heard a voice speaking, "This is My dearly loved Son. You must listen to Him!"

Then, as suddenly as it had come, the vision was gone. They looked around and saw nobody with them except Jesus. On their way back down the hillside He advised them not to tell anybody about what they had seen until after He had risen from the dead. They latched onto that statement and tried to figure out in their own minds what "risen from the dead" meant. So they came up with this question for Jesus:

"Why do the scribes say that Elijah has to come before the Christ?"

"Elijah does come first," He told them, "and begins to prepare the way. But what do the scriptures say about the Son of Man? Just this: that He has to go through a lot of abuse and contempt! Now, you see, Elijah has come already and they have done to him as they pleased—just the way the old scripture predicted they would. The Son of Man will also have to suffer at their hands."

Then they understood that He was talking about John the Baptist and Himself. (*Mark* 9:2-13; *Matthew* 17:1-13; *Luke* 9:28-36)

They were remembering the time, not long before, when John in prison had heard from his own disciples all about the things Jesus was doing and saying. After having preached so positively that he, John, was only the forerunner of the Messiah who would follow, John now wanted reassurance that he had been right in his belief that his cousin, Jesus, was that man. So he had sent some of his own followers to ask Jesus point blank:

"Are You the One who is to come, or shall we look for another?"

Jesus had gone on with the work He was doing when John's messengers arrived. He had continued to heal sick people, restore sight to some blind people, and tend to every need of poor and hurt people which He could meet. And instead of answering John's question with a verbal "Yes" or "No," which would have been only His own word for it, Jesus told them to go back to John and tell him what they had seen Him doing.

"Blind people seeing again, lame people walking again, lepers being cleansed, dead people getting new life, and the humble people having the Good News of God's love being preached to them, are the signs of the Messiah according to the old prophets," Jesus was saying in effect.

"Tell John that the person who recognizes these acts of God's power in me is blessed indeed."

After the messengers had gone back to John, Jesus had continued to talk about John to the people who were crowding around Him.

"Many of you went down to the Jordan wilderness to hear John preach. What did you expect to see, some soft character that was like a reed shaking in the wind, some fellow dressed in nice soft clothes? Well, men dressed in the latest fashion garments are found in the king's court. That wasn't what you went to see. You went to see and hear a prophet. And you did. You saw more than a prophet in John. You saw the one Malachi (3:1) wrote about when he said:

'Behold, I send my messenger to prepare the way before me. . .'

"Now I am telling you that there is no Human Being to date who has been greater than John the Baptist. And yet, one who is least in the kingdom of heaven is greater than he! Like the old prophets, John felt he had to be strong willed enough to force his entrance into God's favor. But the kingdom of God doors open more readily to humble people who simply accept God's love and who realize that the kingdom is theirs through no merit of their own. John preached that the time for the kingdom of God's rule has come, and the lowest of sinners, both men and women, who accepted John's announcement of it, know it is true. Religious leaders who rejected John's baptism of repentance simply rejected the kingdom's approach.

"But to what shall I compare this generation? So many are like children sitting in the village square. Some of them say 'Let's play weddings.' And they act like they are playing the musical pipes, but the other children won't dance. They don't want to play a happy game. Then the children who are trying to get some game started say, 'Let's play funerals.' And they start the funeral crying, but the other children won't act out the weeping. They don't want to play sad games either. They don't want to do anything at all.

"John the Baptist came in an austere way, neither drinking or eating rich foods, and people said 'He is too stern and severe, holding himself aloof from us.' Then I come along enjoying food and drink and they say 'He is a glutton and a drunkard; He mingles with foreign agents and sinners. He doesn't refuse to associate with anybody!'

"So we will just have to look at the results of our ministry and see what good is accomplished!" (*Matthew* 11:2-19; *Luke* 7:18-35)

Jesus called to their remembrance the fact that the cities where most of His greatest works had been done still had not accepted His message and changed their ways.

"If the miraculous things which were done in our ministry in Bethsaida and nearby Chorazin (things which are not found in any of the Gospel accounts, reminding us of how much we don't know about what Jesus said and did) had been done in gentile cities like Tyre and Sidon, they would have repented long ago in sackcloth and ashes! The only thing I can say is this: when the people of Tyre and Sidon are judged by God they will get a more lenient judgment than the people of our cities who had more opportunity to learn and change.

"And just think about Capernaum! Instead of being so high and mighty, it will end up lower than Hades. Sodom would still be standing if the people there had seen the works of God which you have witnessed lately! (*Matthew* 11:20-24; *Luke* 10:13-15)

"But there is a good side to all this. I am thankful to God, the Lord of heaven and earth, that the saving truth of life is often hidden to people who are wise in their own conceit and yet perfectly clear to children and those who are humble enough to learn.

"You can see God and what God wants in me. God has given me the privilege and task of revealing the divine nature in our human life. Any other way, not shown in Me, is inadequate. But it is perfectly plain with any who are open enough to receive what I share of God." (*Matthew* 11:25-27; *Luke* 10:21-22)

"So come to me all of you who are weary of working so hard to find God's will and are weighted down with the rules of religion, and I will give you rest from that. Submit to my way and let me guide you and you will find peace for your souls, because my yoke is measured to fit you to help you bear your burden, not to be a burden to you." (*Matthew* 11:28-30)

All those memories surrounding John the Baptist and Jesus' comments on how people failed to accept either John or Him crowded their minds as they made their way with Jesus back down the hillside to rejoin the other followers. What they found when they got there was an argument between the disciples and some scribes with the people ringed all around them. As soon as some of the people saw Jesus, they ran toward Him excitedly.

"What is the trouble?" Jesus asked them. And one of the men in the crowd answered:

"Master, I brought my son to You because there is an evil spirit in him. Regardless of where he is, this thing gets hold of him without any warning. He falls to the ground grinding his teeth and foaming at the mouth. He can't take much more of it. I asked your disciples to drive it out, but they didn't have the power to do it."

Jesus' reply was to them all, "O how little faith you have! How long do I have to be with you to teach you? Bring the boy here to me."

So they brought the boy, and just as they got there

he had another epileptic seizure and fell writhing to the ground.

"How long has he been like this?" Jesus asked the father.

"Ever since he was a child," the man replied. Sometimes this evil spirit has thrown him into the fire or into the water and has almost killed him. If You can do anything, please take pity on us and help us."

"If you can do anything!" Jesus repeated. "Anything is possible to the person who believes!"

"I do believe," the boy's father burst out. "Help me to believe more."

By this time an even larger crowd was gathering, so Jesus spoke sharply, as if addressing the evil spirit,

"I command you, you stupid spirit, to get out of this boy right now and never go into him again!"

There was a loud scream, and after one terrible convulsion the boy lay dreadfully still. Some of the onlookers gasped, "He is dead." But Jesus bent over, and grabbing him by the hands He lifted the boy up so that he stood on his own feet. Consciousness returned, and the boy was perfectly well.

After everyone had gone home, the disciples asked Jesus why they were not able to drive that evil spirit out of the boy. Jesus answered, "Nothing can heal this kind of thing except prayer." Both *Matthew* and *Luke* add here that Jesus commented that the disciples did not have enough of the kind of faith that a mustard seed has, the kind of faith that is not intimidated by big problems facing its growth; it just believes it will grow bigger and it does. Even problems that seem to be mountains can finally be moved by that kind of faith in God Who constantly creates and recreates. (*Mark* 9:14-29; *Matthew* 17:14-21; *Luke* 9:37-43)

After that Jesus moved across Galilee toward Capernaum. All along the way He was reminding His disciples that He would be taken into custody by the authorities and that they would kill Him. But on the third day after His death He would be alive again. However, they still were not able to understand what He was saying and they even got so they were afraid to ask Him any more questions about it. (*Mark* 9:30-32; *Matthew* 17:22-23; *Luke* 9:43-45)

When they came into Capernaum the tax booths had been set up, as they were twice a year, to collect the temple tax. Every male Jew over twenty years of age had to pay the half-shekel tax to keep the temple in Jerusalem operating. (Inflation had raised the price from a third-shekel in Jeremiah's time.) The tax collectors caught Peter going by one day and asked him whether Jesus ever paid the tax. They would like to catch Him in a violation of the law.

"Of course He does!" Peter responded without batting an eye. But then he hurried to Jesus to ask Him whether He would pay or not.

"First," Jesus said, "I want to ask you a question. Do kings of the earth take tax tribute from their own families, or from other people?"

"From others," Peter answered.

"That's right. The family is free; they don't have to pay the tax. We are God's own family and we don't have to pay taxes to worship in our own family's House. We know that. But, in order not to be a stumbling block to anyone else who might get hurt if they don't pay the tax, we will pay." (Why was this a problem for Matthew's readers? The Jewish temple had already been destroyed by the Romans in 70 A.D. But the Roman emperor, Vespasian, had ordered that all Jews must now pay the half-shekel tax to the temple of Jupiter Capitolinus in Rome. Should they do it? Apparently Jesus' advice would be that they know in their own minds that they are children of God, but as vassals of the Empire they should pay the tax without a fight.)

"Where will I get the money?" Peter wondered.

"You are a fisherman. Go catch fish to sell and then pay the tax for both of us," Jesus advised him. The fish really didn't need to have a coin in its mouth; that part of the story might have been added to make a better fish story. Jesus had already resisted that temptation to use His power to turn stones into bread for personal gain. The story never says, incidentally, whether Peter followed through or not. We assume that he did. (*Matthew* 17:24-27)

After they arrived in Capernaum Jesus opened a discussion with His closest companions by asking, "What were you talking about as we were walking along today?"

Nobody wanted to answer because they had been arguing about which one of them was to be the greatest. So Jesus sat down with them and made it plain:

"If a person wants to be first, that person has to be willing to be last, to be the servant of everybody."

To illustrate the point, He took a little child who was there in the house and stood him up in front of all of them. Jesus put His arms around the child and said to His disciples, "Whoever welcomes one little child like this for my sake is welcoming me. And the person who accepts me, you remember, is really not only accepting me but the One Who sent me!" (*Mark* 9:33-37; *Matthew* 18:1-5; *Luke* 9:46-48)

It was a quiet moment; then John spoke up.

"Master, You know what? Today we saw a man driving out evil spirits in Your name, so we stopped him because he doesn't belong to this group that You have called."

But Jesus' answer was like this: "You ought not to stop him. Nobody who finds that he has power for good in my name is going to say anything against me. If the man is not for us, he is on our side. In fact, anybody who so much as gives you a drink of cold water in my name, because you are followers of mine, is going to be rewarded. And I'll tell you this too—anybody who tries to spoil the faith that one of the poorest followers may have in me would be better if he had tied a great big stone around his neck and was thrown into the sea!'' (*Mark* 9:38-41)

''Temptations are going to come, but you don't want to be the person who brings them to others. And do everything you possibly can to resist any temptation to do evil because your inner self, the real person that lives on beyond this physical life, is more important than even the essential parts of your body like the eye, or hand, or foot.'' (And here both *Mark* and *Matthew* place again Jesus' words which we already read in Matthew's collection of Jesus teachings in the ''Sermon on the Mount,'' in *Matthew* 5:17-30. Likewise, *Mark* recalls here Jesus' saying about salt that has lost its saltiness being no good for anything, which *Matthew* 5:13 and *Luke* 14:34-35 record.)

People who are working hard at being ''religious'' and often unhappy over having to obey so many rules, resent it when ''sinners'' seem to receive benefits from life when they don't deserve them. So why was Jesus spending His time visiting with ''unclean'' people, even having meals with them? The Pharisees and scribes wanted to know one day.

For answer, Jesus first asked two questions with word-pictures to illustrate:

''Is there any man here who owns a hundred sheep who wouldn't go after one of them if it was lost? No, a person would leave the ninety-nine and look for the other one until it was found. Then he would pick it up and carry it home, happy that he had found it. When he gets home, he would spread the good news to family and friends so that they could be glad with him. But that's nothing compared to the joy shared in heaven when one sinner changes, more than for ninety-nine righteous people who don't need changing. (Also *Matthew* 8:10-14)

"Is there any woman here who, if she lost one of her ten silver coins, wouldn't turn on the lights and carefully sweep the floor until she finds it? She'd be so happy, too, that she would let all her family and friends know about her getting back the one coin that was lost. No wonder there is joy among those who are with God when one lost person is recovered for God's family.

"Once there was a man who had two sons. The younger brother was anxious to get his share of the inheritance and go out into the world, so the father divided the estate between the two. Not long after he had turned his share into cash, the younger brother left home for the bright lights of the big city. For a while he was living fast and easy, but his money ran out at the same time that dry weather and hard times hit that part of the country. The only job he could find was one that had him feeding hogs on a farm. Not only was it detestable work for a good Jew, it paid so little that he was hungry enough at times to want to eat the same food the hogs were being fed. But no one would give him any help.

"Then one day he faced up to reality.

"'Back home the hired servants have all they want to eat, and I am over here in this country starving to death! I am going home and I will just admit to my father that I have sinned against God and against him. I'm no longer worthy of being his son, but I will ask just to be treated as one of his hired servants.'

"The decision made, he hit the road for home, but while he was still quite a ways down the road from the house his father saw him coming. Overcome with compassion for the young son, the father ran down the road to meet him. He threw his arms around him and welcomed him. And the son began his little memorized speech which he had turned over in his mind again and again: 'Father, I have sinned against heaven and against you; I am no longer worthy to be called your son, just let me be. . .' But the father interrupted with a command to servants standing nearby: 'Hurry and bring some clean clothes. Put a family ring on his finger and kill the fatted calf for a special barbeque. We are going to have a feast and a party tonight. We are going to celebrate because my son is back home again, like the dead coming to life again, or finding one who was lost.'

"So the party started.

"Now the elder brother was out in the field, working hard 'til dark. Finally, he headed for home. At first, he couldn't believe his ears.

"'What's that noise coming from the house? It sounds like music for a dance.'"

"'It is," one of the servants said. "Your brother has come home, and your father started this celebration because he is safe at home again.'"

"'That's all I need to hear after a hard day's work in the hot sun!' the older brother said. 'I'm not going in there and act like I'm glad to see him.'

"Once again the father left the house, this time to plead with the older son to come and join the party. What he got for his efforts was a tirade from the Number One son:

"'All these years I have stayed here and got the work done, and I've done whatever you wanted me to do, but did you ever once throw a party for me and my friends? No. But when this son of yours comes home after blowing all your money on women and drink, you welcome him back with a steak dinner and dance!'"

"'Son, this is always your home, and everything I have here is yours. You know that. But tonight we have to celebrate because your brother is alive and well and home again!''' (*Luke* 15:11-32)

"That father is a good representative of the kingdom of God."

Willingness to forgive the one who does wrong or breaks relationships with us is the very heart of living with the rule of God's Spirit. Mending broken relationships at whatever cost is priority business, Jesus undoubtedly stressed with His followers. But the little section *Matthew* adds in 18:15-20 are words added for the sake of the church some years after Jesus' time. It may be good practical advice for keeping harmony in a church which would later be established, but it isn't a statement Jesus would have made to His disciples while He was with them: "If another church member sins against you, go talk privately with him and try to work out the problem. If he or she won't listen, take along some witnesses from the group and go back. If the offender still won't listen to reason, take the matter to the whole church meeting. Then, if he or she won't abide by the ruling of the whole church, kick the person out of the church and have absolutely nothing to do with that person.

"What the church binds on earth shall be bound in heaven; and whatever you loose on earth will be loosed in heaven." It sounds as if some church authority is going to have the power to excommunicate a person not only from the association with the church here on earth, but also from any possibility of a saving fellowship in life after death. And the institutional church later did interpret their duty that way. But perhaps Jesus simply stressed how important it is for us to get our relationships straightened out here because they affect our life forever.

"Anything can be worked out if two or three of you agree to give it your most careful and persistent prayer. God will help you work it out. When even just two or three of you are solidly together in my spirit, then you can count on my being there with you." (*Matthew* 18:15-20) *Luke* 17:3 just raises the issue without pursuing it so far.

In fact, *Matthew* 18:21-22 immediately goes much deeper into Jesus' own idea about forgiveness than the church-committee advice just preceding it. Peter put the same question to Him, "Lord, how many times does someone get to sin against me before I stop forgiving? As many as seven times? (That's more than twice the three times our tradition says we must forgive.)"

"How about seventy times seven?" Jesus answered. "Try that."

Luke 17:4 quotes Jesus as saying that "if someone does you wrong seven times a day and each time says 'I'm sorry,' you must keep forgiving."

A story Jesus told fits right here.

"There was a king who wanted to settle accounts with people who had been handling parts of his business for him. One man owed him over two million dollars. He couldn't pay, so the king ordered that everything the debtor had should be sold, including all his personal possessions and even family as slaves, to apply to the debt.

"When the man heard the decision, he fell on his knees before the king and begged for time. 'Give me time, and I will get the money to pay my debt to you.' He pled so earnestly that the king took pity on him and did more than give him extra time; he released him entirely from the debt.

"But that man went out and the first thing he did when he met another man who owed him only five dollars was to grab him by the neck and shake him while he shouted 'Pay what you owe!' That man fell down at his knees, just as he had before the king.

"'Just give me a little more time, and I'll get the

money for you. Please!'"

"'Nothing doing! You're going to jail,' the big money man said without pity.

"Other people who witnessed that display of hardness went to the king and told him the whole story. And once more the original character was brought into the presence of the king.

"'You low-down rascal!' the king began, 'I forgave you all that big debt you owed me because you pled for mercy from me. But you never had one bit of pity for the poor man who owed you a much smaller debt. Now you get the same sentence you had passed on him; you will go to jail till you have paid me back every cent you owe!'"

"How do you think God can forgive each one of you unless you, in turn, forgive from your heart any other who has done you wrong?" (*Matthew* 18:23-35)

This business of accepting others, even when they don't accept us, is not an easy thing to do. At one point in Jesus' ministry, when He had made up His mind to go down to Jerusalem to challenge the religious establishment, *Luke* 9:51-56 reveals that Jesus' own followers had not yet learned the lessons on forgiveness.

Jesus sent messengers ahead of Him to make arrangements for Him and His party to have meals and spend the night in a village of Samaria. But, because He was on His way to hated Jerusalem, the Samaritans would not allow them to stop in their town. When the group heard that news, James and John were burned up, and they wondered if somebody shouldn't burn up that inhospitable village.

"Lord, do you want us to bid fire to come down from heaven and consume them?"

But Jesus rebuked them for even thinking such a thing. "We will just go on to another village," He said.

The three synoptic Gospels tell of Jesus' going to

Jerusalem only once, at the end of His ministry. Obviously He made the journey more than once, probably often as the Gospel of *John* says. The writers did not arrange their stories about Him in chronological order always. If He and His traveling group went only once, then *Luke* and *Mark* have them taking different routes. While *Luke* says they went through Samaria, *Mark* says they avoided Samaria, as most Galileans did, by going down the east side of the Jordan River to cross back into Judea at Jericho.

It didn't matter where He went, crowds gathered around Jesus, *Mark* tells us. And, as always, He taught them. As usual, some of the Pharisees met Him merely to put Him on the spot with this question:

"Is it right for a man to divorce his wife?"

Jesus, in return, put this question to them:

"What was Moses' commandment about this?"

They replied, "Moses said that a man should write out a divorce notice and then he could send her off."

"Moses made that allowance because you men know so little of the meaning of love. From the very first, God created people to be mated. You will remember the scripture says, 'A man shall leave his father and mother and shall become a partner with his wife, and the two shall be like one person.' So, if in fact the man and woman are no longer two people, but one, then no one should separate what God has joined together."

When they got to the place where they were staying that night, His own disciples raised the same question again, and Jesus told them, "Any man who sets aside his own wife with a divorce notice for any reason except adultery and then marries another women, commits adultery against his wife. If she herself divorces him and marries another man, she commits adultery."

In Matthew's version (19:10) the real problem, as far as the men were concerned, surfaces. "If marriage is to be that binding, then a man had better not marry!" Men looked upon marriage as a convenience for them, another way to use women who had no legal rights of their own. But Jesus maintained that women were equal partners in the marriage. They were not the property of men to keep or throw away as they pleased.

Neither should the rights of little children be abridged by adults. Later, some people brought their little children to Him. The disciples tried to stop them before they got to Jesus. Jesus noticed what the disciples were doing and said, "Never stop little children from coming to me. Let them come, because the kingdom of God is made of little ones like these. In fact, any person who enters the kingdom of God must come to it the way a little child does."

Then He picked up each little child and held the child tenderly in His arms. (*Matthew* 19:13-15; *Mark* 10:13-16; *Luke* 18:15-17)

As Jesus set off on His journey again, a man came hurrying up and knelt down before Him saying, "Good Master, will You please tell me what I must do to be absolutely sure of eternal life?"

"I wonder why you call me good," Jesus answered. "Only God is good. You know the commandments, don't you? 'Don't murder, commit adultery, steal, lie or cheat, and honor your father and mother.'"

The man replied, "Master, I have been careful to keep all these commandments all my life."

As Jesus looked quietly at him, He liked what He saw about this young man. Then He said,

"You have failed at only one point. You ought to sell everything you have and give that money away to poor people. That way the only wealth and interests you have will be in heaven, and then come and be one of my disciples."

When he heard this, a look of disappointment crossed the man's face, and he backed off, shaking his head, because he was very rich. Jesus stood and watched him go, then turned to say to His disciples and the people who had overheard the conversation,

"It is certainly hard for people who own a lot of things to enter the kingdom of God!"

The disciples were shocked at these words and their faces showed it, so Jesus continued,

"You just don't realize how hard it can be to get into the kingdom of heaven. You know something? A camel could squeeze through the eye of a needle easier than a rich person can get into the kingdom of God."

Now they were really shocked. All of them had only one question:

"Well, who can possibly get in?"

Jesus looked thoughtfully at them and said,

"It seems impossible to you, but you don't know how to understand all the workings of God."

Then Peter burst out,

"But look at us! We've left everything to follow You."

"Yes, and I promise you this," Jesus came back, "nobody leaves home and family or property in order to follow me and to work for God without getting adequately paid right here in this present world. You will get more meaning out of homes and family and property—even in the midst of sure persecution—and in the next world you will have everlasting life. But many people who seem to have everything now will have nothing then, and some of the people who are at the end of the line now will be moved up to first place. (*Matthew* 19:16-30; *Mark* 10:17- 31; *Luke* 18:18-30)

"When it comes to getting into the kingdom of

heaven, it's like this: A vineyard owner went out early in the morning to hire some laborers for his vineyard. He agreed to give them the regular going wage for a day's work and sent them into the vineyard. But since the harvest had to be gathered quickly before the rains came, the owner went back about nine o'clock to the place where men waited to be hired. Sure enough there were more, so he hired them too.

"Go on out to my field, and I will give you what is right at the end of the day."

It just happened that he was able to pick up a few more workers at noon and then again about three o'clock. Each time he asked them "Do you want to just sit around here, or do you want to work?"

They all told him, "We want to work, but nobody has hired us yet."

"Well, I've got work to be done. Get out to my vineyard and get with it."

He even hired a few more about five o'clock.

When dark came, the owner had the field boss call all the men in to collect their pay. "Start with the ones I hired last and pay them first, then work back down the line to the ones I hired early this morning," he told the paymaster.

The men hired at five o'clock were overjoyed to get a full day's wage. So were the ones who started to work in the afternoon earlier. Seeing all this, the ones who were hired first in the morning thought they would get more because they had worked longer. But when they stepped up for pay, they got the regular wage for a day's work just as the others had.

"Wait a minute," they grumbled, "this isn't fair. These other workers only put in a part of the day, but we worked in the heat all day long!"

The owner was ready with this reasoning:

"Am I doing wrong by you? I promised to give you a regular day's wage for your work, and you agreed to come and work. So take what belongs to you. If I choose to pay these men I hired last the same wage, how is that doing you an injustice? Am I not allowed to do what I want with my money? Or do you get angry because I choose to be generous?'' (*Matthew* 20:1-16)

It was a lesson that was not wasted on the disciples who had signed up first to follow Jesus and who had to watch while those who had only recently joined were treated equally well by Jesus. And it was a lesson church members have needed to consider ever since that day.

Challenge to Jerusalem

Continuing on their way to Jerusalem, Jesus walked on ahead. The disciples were nervous, and others in the crowd of His followers were afraid because Jesus had taken the twelve aside and told them some of the things that would happen to Him.

"As you can see, we are going up to Jerusalem. I will be betrayed there into the hands of the chief priests and scribes. They will condemn me to death, and hand me over to the Romans who will make fun of me, beat me, and kill me. But after three days I will come back to life." (*Matthew* 20:17-19; *Mark* 19:32-34; *Luke* 18:31-34)

Was it James and John, the Zebedee boys, or was it their mother who made a request of Jesus in their behalf? *Matthew* says the mother brought up the subject; *Mark* says the two brothers tried to get Jesus to agree to do what they asked.

"What do you want me to do for you?" Jesus inquired.

"When You come into power in Your kingdom, let us be the ones to sit on either side of you!"

"You don't know what you are asking," Jesus told them. "Will you be able to stand up to all the trouble I will have to endure? Will you actually be able to make the complete sacrifice that I will have to make?"

"Sure we can," they said.

Then Jesus made it clear. "It is certain that you will

have to stand up under the time of testing and go through the same kind of treatment which I must endure! But as to granting your request to sit in the special places of honor in the kingdom of God, that is not for me to give. God will handle that."

The other ten disciples got pretty angry at John and James for trying to get the places of honor, so Jesus had to gather them all together to remind them again,

"You all know that in this world the people who are the so-called rulers always have to show who's boss, and insist that everybody knows who has the position and the power. It shouldn't be that way with you. In fact, if one of you wants to become great, that one has to be the servant of everybody. If someone wants to be in a special position of honor, that one must put everybody else ahead of him or herself. For I did not come to be served, did I? No, I came to serve, and to give my life so that others may live."

The journey took them through Jericho, and as they were moving through town one man seemed determined to get a good look at this man the crowd was surrounding. He was the chief tax collector for Jericho, a Jew who was despised for the riches he had gained, but he was also too short in stature to see over the other people who lined the streets. So he ran on ahead and climbed into a sycamore tree so that he could see Jesus when He passed by.

Not only could he see Jesus from his perch in the tree, Jesus could see him, and when He got under the tree He paused and said, "Zacchaeus, why don't you come on down? I would like to stay at your house today."

Zacchaeus almost fell out of the tree in his haste to get down to lead Jesus and His group to his residence. He was as amazed as the orthodox Jews were that a religious leader like Jesus would actually enter the house of an "unclean" sinner like him. By now the strict Jews were murmuring among themselves.

"Did you see that? He has gone in to be the guest of a man who is a big sinner?"

When they were all settled inside, Zacchaeus stood and welcomed them and then added to Jesus, "Lord, I am saying right now that I am going to give half my goods to the poor. And if I have cheated any one of any amount, I will restore it to that person fourfold."

Evidently Jesus felt that a person's changed attitude about money and material possessions is a good key to the new condition of his or her soul because His answer to Zacchaeus was a definite assurance of His approval,

"Today salvation has come to this house! After all," Jesus added to the onlookers, "Zacchaeus is also a son of Abraham. And I came to find and to save the lost." (*Luke* 19:1-10)

As they were leaving town later, the large crowd of people was following Jesus as usual. Along the roadside a blind man named Bartimaeus was seated and begging alms of passersby. (*Matthew* says there were two blind beggars sitting together.) When he heard that it was the famous Jesus of Nazareth going by, Bartimaeus started shouting,

"Jesus, Son of David, take pity on me!"

The people around him told him to keep quiet but he yelled even louder,

"Son of David, take pity on me!"

Jesus stopped and said to those near Him, "Tell the blind man to come here."

So they called Bartimaeus, "It's O.K. now. You can come on; He's asking for you."

Bartimaeus jumped to his feet, leaving his coat behind, and felt his way toward Jesus.

"What do you want me to do for you?" Jesus asked.

"Oh, Master, I want to see again. You can heal me!"

"All right," returned Jesus, "you can go on your way seeing because your faith has healed you."

And Bartimaeus immediately got his sight back and followed Jesus down the road praising God. Everybody who saw what had happened joined him in his excitement. (*Matthew* 20:29-34; *Mark* 10:46-52; *Luke* 18:35-43)

Still on the road Jesus and His friends were passing ten lepers who stood off the road but called loudly so Jesus could hear them, "Jesus, Master, please have mercy on us!"

Jesus stopped and spoke to them. "Go show yourselves to the priests who can certify that you are clean of leprosy."

Without hesitation they headed for town, and as they went they were healed. One of them, when he saw what was happening, turned back. Running toward Jesus, shouting "Praise God, thank God," he fell on his face at Jesus' feet and overflowed with thanks. Jesus had a question for His followers: "Weren't there ten healed? Where are the other nine? This man is a Samaritan. Was there no one else who would return to give thanks to God except this foreigner?"

Then to the man He said, "You can get up and go on your way; your faith has made you well."

On toward Jerusalem they went with tension building. Along the side of the Mount of Olives the road near Jerusalem passed through the two villages of Bethphage and Bethany. There in Bethany a homemaker named Martha had invited Jesus to be her guest for a meal. While Martha was busy getting everything ready for supper, her sister, Mary, sat in the living room and listened to Jesus talk.

Martha couldn't stand it; she interrupted Jesus' conversation to say to Him:

"Doesn't it make any difference to You that my

sister is leaving all the work to me while she just sits here with You? Tell her to help me."

Jesus' answer was calm. "Martha, Martha, you are so busy and anxious about serving the meal perfectly, but that isn't the most important thing about our time together, is it? Let Mary stay here and learn." (*Luke* 10:38-42)

Jesus knew what kind of entrance He was going to make into Jerusalem and He had already planned to have a donkey ready for the trip of the last mile into the city. The password was set.

"Go into the next village," Jesus told two of His disciples, "and just as you start into the village you will find a donkey colt tied up." (Again *Matthew* says there were two donkeys there, just as there had been two blind men instead of one at Jericho. Once again he misread an Old Testament verse, *Zechariah* 9:9, which said:

"Behold your king is coming to you,
humble and mounted on an ass,
on a colt, the foal of an ass."

Matthew forgot the Hebrew poetry repeated itself, so he counted two animals, which would have made Jesus a trick rider coming into town on two at the same time.)

"If anyone tries to stop you from taking the donkey," Jesus continued, "then you tell them 'The Lord has need of it.' That's the password, and he will let you have the donkey immediately."

When the two men got to the village they found a colt tied to the doorway of a house, and they untied it. Sure enough, the people at the house asked them why they were taking their colt, but as soon as they told them what Jesus had said they gave them permission to take it. Back where Jesus was waiting, they got the donkey ready for His ride. They put some of their coats on the donkey's back for a saddle and Jesus got on. Now He would come as kings came into a capital city when they came in peace, riding on a donkey. Only the conquerors came on horseback or in a chariot.

As the mounted Jesus and the large procession of people made their way down the hillside toward the city gate, some of His followers spread their cloaks on the road. Others cut leafy branches and placed them in the road ahead of the donkey. The symbolism of the whole event was obvious to all who knew their scripture; this was the coming of the Messiah to the holy city. So excitement bred more excitement and people along the route picked up the chant begun by His followers.

"Hosanna!" they sang or shouted. "Blessed be the One who comes in the name of the Lord! Hooray for the kingdom of our father David which is returning. Blessed be the Lord!" (*Matthew* 21:1-9; *Mark* 11:1-10; *Luke* 19:28-38)

The first readers of the Gospels would have had no trouble in imagining what apprehension a procession like that would have caused among the authorities in the capital city. Roman security forces were always on the lookout for anything that might turn a demonstration into a riot or even a revolution. The Jewish leaders, who knew how heavy-handed and cruel the Romans could be if they felt some group was challenging their rule, were anxious to keep anyone from rocking the political boat. So when the Pharisees heard the followers of Jesus shouting nationalist slogans that implied the kingdom of David was going to be restored, they hastened to quiet the demonstration before the Romans thought a serious threat was developing.

"Teacher, stop Your people from shouting those things!"

"Listen," Jesus answered, "I tell you that if these

people were silent now, the very stones would cry out."

As they came to the gates of the city itself, Jesus had tears in His eyes. This was to be His last attempt to get Jerusalem to accept His message, and He knew that it was doomed to failure. The enthusiasm of the crowd with Him would not be shared by everyone in the city.

"If only you knew today the things that make for real peace!" Jesus said as if to the city in front of Him. "But you can't see them." And thinking of what their reliance on political scheming and military action would bring Israel soon, He prophesied that "the days will come when Jerusalem again will be in a state of seige, with the troops of the Empire surrounding it. The city will be destroyed and everybody in it. The whole city will be leveled, blotted out—all because you don't know that God is appealing to you now through me." (*Luke* 19:39-44)

When Jesus and the shouting crowd poured into the streets of the city, the whole city was aroused. People were asking "Who is this? What's going on?"

And others who knew were saying "This is the famous prophet Jesus, from Nazareth in Galilee."

Straight to the temple they went. Jesus looked all around at what was going on there. Then, since it was already late in the afternoon, He and His closest disciples went back to Bethany to spend the night. Probably his good friends Martha, Mary and Lazarus had made arrangements for them there.

The next morning when He started back down the hillside to enter Jerusalem Jesus spotted a fig tree near the road. It was full-leafed and inviting, but when He went over to it to pick fruit, according to the stories in both *Mark* and *Matthew*, He found no fruit on it. *Mark* explains that it wasn't the season for figs to be ripe there. Jesus knew He would find no figs there to eat, but here was a tree He could use to act out a parable the way the old prophets of Israel did it. This tree, in full leaf, obviously was not going to bear figs at all that year. And a fig tree that is all show and no fruit is not worth keeping alive. Could the people with Him not see that a nation which is all talk about the God of Love but is not producing the fruits of love is exactly like that tree?

In effect, Jesus said to the tree, "You've had it! You will never produce again."

The next day He would build on that idea when they passed the tree again.

So they went on into Jerusalem and back to the temple. There Jesus wasted no time in doing one thing He had come there to do. When the first money-changing table was thrown over, a shock wave ran through the temple court where people were busy buying and selling merchandise, especially religious paraphenalia. The shock turned into an uproar as Jesus continued upsetting tables, knocking over pigeon and dove cages. It angered Him to see how poor pilgrims were exploited by the money changers who exacted the temple tax from them, and who made big profits changing the people's regular money into "sacred" money which was the only currency allowed in the temple area.

Also, the merchants of the high priest's family were selling officially-approved birds at outlandish prices since they allowed no other birds to be used as sacrifices.

Nor could Jesus tolerate the fact that it was the outer "court of the gentiles" that was filled with all the traffic and business of a city market.

"This part of the temple is supposed to be a place of worship for all people of all nations," Jesus shouted. "You make it over into a den of thieves!"

The chief priests and other temple officials would

have reacted right away, but what could they do when Jesus obviously had the backing of His rugged followers plus the approval of the people who had long complained about being victimized by the temple's corrupt system? The people listened eagerly all day to the One who had struck this courageous blow in their behalf, but the officials plotted to get rid of Him forever.

For the next four days of the week, as Jesus and His close followers would enter and leave the city each day, the enthusiasm of the crowds that gathered around Him in the temple court kept the authorities at bay. (*Matthew* 21:10-17; *Mark* 11:11-19; *Luke* 19:45-48)

The next morning, returning to the city from Bethany, the fig tree story gets finished. That tree which Jesus had branded "worthless" was withering. The disciples nearest Him thought that this surely was a great demonstration of "power" on Jesus' part. Jesus took their wonder as another opportunity to stress how much a clear, complete faith in God can produce. Once again He repeats an illustration He used often, just as some of the great Rabbis did in their teaching. "You could move mountains (any problem or difficulty) if you had enough faith. All the resources of the limitless Creator God are with you when you line up your will with God's will perfectly. And when you pray be sure that your spirit is completely forgiving, with no shred of resentment toward any person, so that God may forgive you completely and open the channels of power for life." (*Matthew* 21:20-22; *Mark* 11:20-25)

When they got back to the temple again, the officials were ready with the standard administrative question, "Where do You get the authority to do what You are doing? Who gave You permission?"

"Let me ask you a question," Jesus replied, "and

if you will answer me then I will answer your question. I will tell you where I get the authority for what I have to do. Now, my question to you is about the baptism of John. Did it come from heaven, or was it only human? Tell me that."

That got them. As they whispered together about how to answer, they realized that if they said that it came from heaven, Jesus would say "Then, why didn't you believe in him?" But if they said it was purely human, they would turn all the people against them, because they all believed that John was a real prophet. So they had to answer,

"We don't know."

"Then I cannot tell you by what authority I do my work," Jesus answered. (*Matthew* 21:23-27; *Mark* 11:27- 33; *Luke* 20:1-8)

Jesus continued by telling some stories.

"What do you think about this? A man had two sons; and he went to the first one and said 'Son, I need you to go into the vineyard today and work.' The son answered, 'No, I won't go.' But afterward he felt ashamed that he had said 'No' to his father, so he went out and did the work.

"Meanwhile, the father had gone to the other son with the same request for help. That son said immediately, 'Sure, father, I will go.' But he never did go to do the work.

"Now which one of these two did the will of his father?" Jesus asked His hearers.

Of course, they said "the first one."

"That's right," Jesus acknowledged, "and that is why I tell you that the tax collectors and harlots will go into the kingdom of heaven ahead of you religious leaders here. John came to you preaching the way of righteousness, and you didn't believe him; but the tax collectors and harlots believed him and they repented. Even after you saw that happen, you didn't think again and repent yourselves.'' (*Matthew* 21:28-32)

He followed that story with this one.

''A man planted a vineyard one time. He built a fence around it, dug a big hole for a wine press, and built a platform for overseeing the whole vineyard. Before he took a trip out of the country, he rented his vineyard to some sharecroppers. At the end of that season, he sent one of his servants back to get his share of the earnings from the tenants. But the men on the farm beat up the servant and sent him back without anything.

''The owner tried again. He sent another servant back, but again they insulted the servant and beat him up. A third time the owner sent a man to collect his rent, and this time the farm workers actually killed him. It was the same way with several others the owner sent; some they beat up and sent home empty-handed, and some they killed. Finally, he had only one man left, his own son whom he loved more than anyone else. He decided to send him because he thought the tenants surely would respect his own son.

''But when the son arrived, the tenants said to each other, ''Here is the future owner. If we get rid of him, everything will come to us. Come on. Let's kill him!'' So they jumped on him and murdered him and threw his body out of the vineyard.

''What do you think the owner of that vineyard is going to do? He will come and put to death the men who did all this, and he will turn the vineyard over to others. Don't you remember the scripture. . .

'The stone that was rejected by the builders
Has been made the head cornerstone;
This was the work of the Lord,
And it is marvelous to see it done?'''

The priests and scribes knew that Jesus aimed that story at them. *Matthew* even adds for readers like us who weren't there, ''Therefore, the kingdom of God will be taken away from you and given to people who will be worthy of it.'' And *Luke* comments that anyone who tries to break that cornerstone of God will be broken by it. So the temple authorities would have liked to have their men take Jesus right then; but they were afraid of the people, so they waited for a better time. (*Matthew* 21:33-46; *Mark* 12:1-12; *Luke* 20:9-19)

Here *Matthew* adds another parable Jesus told which conveyed the same message to the Jerusalem establishment. *Luke* put a similar story earlier in his accounts.

''Let's look at the kingdom of heaven this way,'' Jesus said. ''A king gave a big marriage feast for his son and sent his servants out to tell those who had been invited that it was time to come. But nobody would come.

'''Maybe we have to be a little more specific,' the king thought. 'Tell them that the meat is all cooked, and everything is ready now for the dinner. They should come immediately.'

''Still the invited guests ignored the call. They went about their own business. One went out to his farm to check something; others actually mistreated the king's servants who had come to urge them to get over to the dinner party. And some were so angered by the king's persistence that they killed the messengers he sent. That was a bad mistake, and their last one. The king sent soldiers the next time, not to invite them again to dinner but to put to death the murderers who had killed his servants. (*Matthew* even says 'They burned their city'— since Jerusalem had been burned and destroyed before this was written in final form.) Now the king had other plans. Calling other servants together, he told them,

'I have this banquet ready and it is not going to waste! Go out in the streets and invite everybody you can find to come and enjoy it.'

"When word of that open invitation got around, the dining hall soon filled up with people of all kinds. But none of those invited originally were allowed to come." (*Matthew* 22:1-10; *Luke* 14:16-24)

So the door to the banquet which symbolizes the kingdom of heaven is now open to all people of all nations. It is no longer exclusively Jewish, but when people come to it they still have the personal responsibility of preparing themselves to take part in it. Their old ways have to be exchanged for new, hands and face washed and clothes changed. *Matthew* makes that plain by adding verses 11-14 to the story in chapter 22.

"But when the king came in to look at the guests, he saw one man there who had not washed or put on a suitable garment for the wedding feast.

"'How did you get in here without cleaning up and dressing properly?' the king asked.

"The man didn't know how to reply. He was just there as a freeloader, not to participate in the wedding celebration.

"'Throw him out,' the king ordered his servants. 'Everybody is invited, but not everybody actually becomes a part of the heaven group. The H.B.s who aren't willing to prepare themselves may cry and grind their teeth forever because they are missing the banquet, but they can't take part in it until they are prepared to meet the requirements.'"

Later that day, the opposition leaders had another plan. They sent some Pharisees and some members of Herod's party (a sure sign that they were ganging up on Him since these two groups were normally enemies). They had cooked up an argument that they thought would trap Him.

"Master, we know that you say what you think and that you are not swayed by people's opinion of you.

It is obvious that you teach the way of God and stick strictly to the truth, regardless of what people think. Is it right to pay tribute to Caesar or not? Should we pay or not?''

Jesus saw what they were up to and said to them, ''Why are you trying this trick on me? Bring me a coin and let's look at it.''

So someone handed Him a coin.

''Whose face is this on the coin?'' Jesus asked, ''and whose name is this printed here?''

''Caesar's,'' they answered.

''Then give to Caesar what belongs to Caesar, and give to God what belongs to God.''

They couldn't get around that answer. (*Matthew* 22:15-22; *Mark* 12:13-17; *Luke* 20:20-26)

As they faded away, some Sadducees (a group of powerful religious leaders who did not believe in life after death) came up to Jesus with another question they thought would trap Him.

''Master, the book of Moses tells us that if a man dies leaving a widow but no child, the man's brother is supposed to marry the woman and raise a family for his brother. Now, let's say that there were seven brothers and the first one marries and dies without having any children. Then a second one marries the widow, and also dies without children. The same thing happens with the third, and so on down the line through the whole seven. Finally, the woman herself dies. Now, if there is a 'resurrection' when people come to life again, whose wife is she going to be?''

Jesus noted the smug look on their faces as He answered, ''Perhaps this shows where you are mistaken and where you are ignorant of both the scriptures and the power of God. When people rise from the dead in the next life they don't marry as people do in this world; they live in a spiritual existence. And as far as the dead being raised is concerned, haven't you read in the story of Moses when Moses was at the burning bush how God spoke to him in these words, 'I am the God of Abraham, Isaac and Jacob?' God is not God of the dead, but of the living. This is the point you miss."

Once again the crowd was astonished at the way Jesus handled such issues. One of the lawyers who had been listening to all this discussion and observing how well Jesus answered them all put his question to Jesus:

"Which of all the commandments is the greatest?"

"How do you read the law?" Jesus turned the question back on the man.

"You shall love the Lord your God with all your heart, and with all your soul, and with all your mind, and with all your strength; and the second one is like it, you shall love your neighbor as yourself."

"That's exactly right," Jesus said. "Do that and you will live. There is no commandment greater than these. All the law and the prophets hang on these two."

"You're absolutely right," the lawyer agreed. "We ought to love God with all our heart and intelligence and energy, and we ought to love our neighbors as ourselves. This is a whole lot more important than all these sacrifices and burnt offerings here in the temple!"

Jesus realized how thoughtfully the lawyer answered, so He said to him, "You are mighty close to the kingdom of God."

A profound silence spread over the crowd, and nobody felt like asking Him any more questions. (*Matthew* 22:23- 38; *Mark* 12:18-34; *Luke* 20:27-40, 10:25-28)

Luke has a different ending to the incident.

"The lawyer, looking for an excuse for his own lack

of positive service to others, said to Jesus, 'And who is my neighbor?'

Jesus answered with a story.

"A man was going down the road from Jerusalem to Jericho. A bunch of thieves jumped him. They took everything he had, including his clothes, and left him half-dead beside the road. It just happened that a priest was going down the road a little later, but when he saw the wounded man he passed by him on the other side of the road. Soon after, a Levite came on the scene, but he didn't want to get involved either.

"The next traveler that day was a man from Samaria. Just as soon as he saw the wounded man lying beside the road he hurried to him and began to give him first aid. He used oil and wine to clean his wounds, and made bandages of part of his clothing. Carefully, he lifted the beaten victim to the back of his own donkey, then walked them to the nearest inn where he rented a room and put the man to bed. All night he nursed the Jew with whom he would not normally socialize, and when he had to continue his business trip the next day he made arrangements for the innkeeper to take care of the injured man until he returned.

"'Take good care of him, and whatever expenses you have, plus the rent for the room, I will pay you when I come back,' the Samaritan promised before he left.

"Now, which one of these three passers-by proved to be a neighbor to the man who was nearly killed by the robbers?" Jesus asked, as He broke off the story right there.

"Obviously," the lawyer replied, "the one who showed mercy and helped the man in need."

"So, you go and do the same. Anyone in need is your neighbor."

The question: "Who is my neighbor?" can't be

asked with the intent of finding who isn't. The "great commandment" includes everybody a lawyer learned that day. (*Luke* 10:29-37)

During the day while Jesus was teaching in the temple, He had this to say about the religious lawyers, "They have it all figured out that Christ is the son of David. Yet it was David himself who was inspired one time to say 'God said to my Lord (speaking of the Christ), 'You sit on my right hand until I have conquered all your enemies.'

"So, if David himself calls the Christ his 'Lord,' where do the scribes get the idea that He is David's son?"

There was a big crowd listening, and they really liked to hear Jesus be so outspoken against the pious and strict religious leaders. Their feelings were with Him when He said to them,

"Listen to what the Pharisees and scribes tell you, but be careful not to do what they do, because they don't practice what they preach. Have you noticed how some of them love to strut around in long robes? You'd better be sure to give them proper respect in public and let them have the front seats in the synagogues by all means. And of course they must have the best places at the dinner parties! They live on money which they demand from poor widows and others, but then they put up a smokescreen of lengthy prayers, thinking they can hide their selfish desires. But God will take all that into account and will deal with them someday. (*Matthew* 23:1-15; *Mark* 12:37b-40; *Luke* 20:45-47)

"Better watch out, scribes and Pharisees, you hypocrites! You will go anywhere in the world to make a single convert, but when that person becomes like you he or she is not introduced to heaven but to hell.

"Better watch out, you blind guides! You say that

if anyone swears by the temple that oath isn't binding, but if anyone swears by the gold of the temple that person is bound by that oath. How foolish can you get? Which is greater, the gold or the temple that made the gold sacred? And you say that if anyone swears by the altar, it doesn't count; but if anyone swears by the gift that is on the altar, then that person is bound to keep that oath. I ask you again, which is greater, the gift on the altar or the altar that makes the gift sacred?

"Actually, when it comes to swearing, when you swear by the altar you swear by everything on it; when you swear by the temple you swear by it and by God Who dwells in it; and when you swear by heaven, you swear by the throne of God and by God Who sits on it.

"You've got trouble coming to you, you scribes and Pharisees, hypocrites! You carefully tithe even mint and dill and cummin, but you are not careful at all about the really important matters of the law of God, justice and mercy and faith. These ought to be your real concerns, and you can still keep your tithing as well. But magnifying such small matters of the religious law while ignoring the weightier matters is like straining a gnat out of your soup while you are swallowing a camel.

"You will have to pay for your hypocrisy! You are careful to clean up the outside of the cup and plate, but leave them dirty inside. Carefully clean outside, you are full of corruption and selfish motives inside. You blind Pharisees, first give your attention to cleaning up your inner selves, then your outward appearance will be clean too.

"But right now you are like whitewashed tombs. The outside of the tombs are clean and shiny, but inside they are full of bones and rottenness. You are such hypocrites that you take care of the tombs of the prophets and carefully decorate the monuments to them, and you say that if you had lived in the days of our ancestors you would not have joined the crowds in opposing the prophets and killing them. You admit that you are the sons of those people, and you are no different. Now you are plotting to keep that tradition going!

"All through Israel's history, the prophets of God have been persecuted and murdered. You are willing to perpetuate that history in whipping and even killing God's spokespersons today. Go ahead, but the blood of all those innocent people from the first man, Abel, to Zechariah, who was stoned to death in the temple court (*II Chronicles* 24:20-21), will be on your hands. Zechariah had died saying, 'May the Lord see and avenge!' Now it will all be avenged on this generation." (*Matthew* 23:15-36; *Luke* 11:42-51)

"You lawyers are busy keeping the rules of the Kingdom of God, but you won't enter it. Even worse, you make it hard for anyone else to enter. You have all this information, but hold back the key of knowledge of what it all means!"

Now more defensive than ever, the lawyers and Pharisees kept trying to provoke Jesus into saying something that would make Him guilty by their law. But the people gathered by the thousands to hear Him. And He told them plainly that they must be careful not to let the temptation to put on a religious show become more important to them than being honest with God, themselves and others. That "leaven" of the Pharisees rises easily within us.

Jesus' anger at the hypocrisy of the religious leaders who led their people astray from God's wholesome way was the other side of the coin of His great compassion for the people of His frustrated and tragic nation. *Matthew* and *Luke* remember the anguish with which He spoke (though they place the saying at two different times and places) with which He spoke when He said, "O Jerusalem, Jerusalem, killing the prophets and stoning those who are sent to you! How often I have wanted to care for you the way a mother hen cares for her chicks, but you wouldn't let me! Now your city is going to be left desolate, and you will never see me again until you are ready to admit that I come in the name of the Lord." (*Matthew* 23:37-39; *Luke* 13:34-35)

Once during that last week Jesus took a seat near the offering box in the temple and watched people putting their money in. Some of the rich people dropped in large amounts. Then a poor widow came up and put in just two little coins. Both of them together would amount to about a penny.

And Jesus had this to say to His disciples,

"You see that poor widow? She just gave more than all the others put together. They all dropped in money they could easily get along without, but she is so poor and needs so much. Yet she has given away the only money she actually has to live on." (*Mark* 12:41-44; *Luke* 21:1-4)

Preparation for Persecution

That day when Jesus was leaving the temple, His disciples were admiring the great size of the building. "Just look at that magnificent stonework," one of them said.

"Yes, these buildings look as if they would last forever," Jesus said, "but they will all be torn down. There will not be a single stone left standing on another one."

Outside of Jerusalem on the Mount of Olives, when they were looking back at the temple, Peter, James, John and Andrew were still wondering about that statement.

Once when He was teaching, a woman in the crowd spoke up, "Your mother who gave birth to You and nursed You is certainly blessed!"

"The people who are really blessed are those who hear the word of God and obey it!" Jesus added. (*Luke* 11:27-28)

"How can we tell when this is going to happen?"

Jesus made this answer. "You'll have to be very careful that no one deceives you. Many men are going to come, claiming they are the leaders you should follow. They will say 'I am the Christ returned.' And a whole lot of people will follow them, I'm sorry to say. When there is talk about war, and when wars actually come, don't be too alarmed. These things are bound to happen, but that doesn't mean the world is coming to an end just yet.

"There will be fighting between nations, and there will be earthquakes and famine here and there; but these are only the birth pains of a new world being born. You yourselves must not get excited or afraid, for you will be severely tested. Men will drag you into their courts, and they will beat you up in their synagogues. You will find yourselves standing in front of government officers and kings, because you are followers of mine. This will be your chance to give your witness—for before the end of the world comes, the gospel must be spread to all nations. When the time comes that they do take you off to trial, don't worry about what you ought to say. Just say whatever comes into your mind when the time comes, because the Holy Spirit will inspire you to say the right thing.

"The time of persecution will be horrible enough. Even families will be divided. One brother will betray another brother, and a father will accuse his own child. Children will condemn their own parents and send them to their death. The whole world will seem to hate you simply because you are known to be my followers. Yet the ones who hold out to the end will be saved. And before the end comes, this gospel of the kingdom of God will be preached throughout the whole world so that all nations will know about it."

Then Jesus, remembering the time of the writing of *Daniel* when the altar of Zeus was built by Antiochus on the site of the Jew's altar of the burnt offering, used a description *Daniel* wrote (9:27). If Jesus was predicting the complete destruction of Jerusalem by the Romans in 70 A.D., including the destruction of the temple, His description of that terrible time is a good picture of what actually happened.

"You will see 'the abomination of desolation' that *Daniel* mentioned set up again. Then those who are outside the city in Judea should flee to the mountains. The person on top of the house should not take time to go down into the house to get anything out of it. One in the field shouldn't stop long enough to pick up a coat. Too bad for women who are pregnant at that time, and too bad for mothers with little babies! You'd better pray that it won't be winter when this time comes, because there will be more terrible misery than in any day since creation—and there probably won't be anything worse again. In fact, if it were not that God has planned for some chosen people to live through it, then no human being would survive those days. (*Matthew* 10:17-25; 24:4-22; *Mark* 13:5-20; *Luke* 21:8-24)

"If anyone tells you then, 'Here comes the Christ!' or 'Look, there is the Christ!' don't you believe it! For there will be those who attempt to deceive the people, even those who truly worship God, and they will claim to be prophets or even Christ. Some of them will seem to have a lot of power and will be quite convincing. But I am warning you now before it happens, that you will have to keep your eyes open!

"But there will be a time when the earth is ready for it, when the sun and moon will fail to give light and the stars are falling, and all the physical universe is upset. Then the Son of Man will return. His angel messengers will call the faithful together from every corner of earth and heaven.

"Let the fig tree illustrate what I am saying to you. When its branches begin to produce leaves, you know that summer is near. So when you see the things happening that I have described to you, it is a sign that the old order is breaking up and the new is coming in. And you can expect this terrible change in your own lifetime! (Was He referring again to the destruction of Jerusalem and the complete crushing of the Jewish nation by Rome?)

"When it comes to the return of the Son of Man and the end of the world as we know it, nobody knows when that will happen. Not the angels, not even the Son Himself—only God knows that! So you just have to keep your eyes open and be alert all the time. Always be on ready for God's visit!

"Think about it like this: A master of an estate leaves his servants to manage until he gets back. He gives each one a job to do, and he tells the doorkeeper to be on the lookout for his return. He wants everything in ship shape when he comes in the door. Well, just so you must keep a lookout always, because you don't know when the Master of Life will visit you. It may be evening, or midnight, or dawn or during the day; but keep expecting Him or He might come and catch you asleep. And what I am saying to you now, I am saying to everybody—always be ready for God! (*Matthew* 24:23-36; *Mark* 13:21-37; *Luke* 17:23-24; 19:12-13, 38, 40)

"You just be sure that you don't get so involved in the cares of this life that the day of spiritual judgment will come on you like a trap springing, for it does come to all persons. But be ready at all times, praying that you will have strength enough to face up to all that will take place and can stand tall before the Son of Man. (*Luke* 21:34-36)

"Remember that in the days of Noah everybody went right on eating and drinking and living their normal lives up to the very day of the flood. Noah (who was ready) got in the ark, but all the others were swept away. That is the way it is going to be when the Son of Man returns. It was that way in the days of Lot also. People were caught by the fire and brimstone while they were giving attention only to the things of their everyday life. Remember Lot's wife who lost her life because she was not willing to turn her back on the lifestyle God wanted her to leave.

"Two men will be in a field together; one will be accepted as part of the kingdom of Heaven and one will be left. Two women will be at work grinding their grain; one will be accepted and one won't.

"Just keep on the lookout every day, and never get so caught up in the affairs of this world and this time that you are not ready for eternity. None of us knows when we will be called away. So live every day as if it were your last, and one day you will be right.

"If a homeowner knew when a thief was coming to the house, the owner would be ready and would not let the thief get in. So you stay alert because you don't know when God's final judgment will come."

Peter interrupted, "Lord, are You saying this to us privately, or is this aimed at everybody?"

"To anyone who wants to be a good steward, one God can trust to take care of the household," Jesus replied, and continued with this illustration (*Luke* 12:41-42):

"If a wealthy employer gives an employee charge of taking care of all the affairs of the household before the employer goes away for a time, and if the owner comes back and finds that everything is in order, then that employee is rewarded with a promotion. But if the person left in charge of the household thinks, 'The boss is gone for a long time,' and so begins to mistreat those under him and wastes the estate's resources by throwing drinking parties, there is going to be a time of rude awakening when the owner comes back unexpectedly. That employee will be kicked out in disgrace. (*Matthew* 24:37-51; *Luke* 12:35-46; and parts of 17:26-37)

"If a slave knows what the master wants him to do, but doesn't prepare to do it, the slave will be punished severely. But if a slave does something wrong, not deliberately disobeying the master, he will get off with light punishment. It's a fact of life that everyone who is given much will be required to account for it. When people put a lot of their trust in a person, they expect more from that person. (*Luke* 12:47-48)

"Remember that we are servants, not the Master. You know that if any person here has a servant who has been plowing or taking care of the sheep all day, you still expect the servant to prepare supper for you. You don't expect the servant to come in and sit down at the table with you, waiting to be served. And you don't especially thank the servant for doing what you order him or her to do. So you, when you have done everything you have been commanded to do, should still admit 'We are just servants, and we have only done our duty.'" (*Luke* 17:7-10)

Jesus stressed this point of being ready at every moment to have your life examined by the Giver of Life. The person who is ready at any moment for more life and growth will get it. The person who isn't may lose what she or he has.

"Being ready for the kingdom of Heaven is like this," Jesus said once. "Ten young women took their lamps and went to be a part of a marriage procession. Five of them were smart enough to take along extra oil for their lamps, but five of them did not. They all knew the custom of the day that the groom may be hours, if not a couple of days, late, and sure enough he was. As the night wore on, they all fell asleep, but after midnight a man came down the street announcing that the groom was ready.

'Come out and go to the marriage feast with the groom,' he was shouting. And all the women shook themselves awake and checked their lamps.

"Oh, no!" said the five who didn't take extra oil. "Our lamps are about to go out. Give us some of yours," they pled with the five who were prepared.

"We may all run short then," the answer came back. "You go to the store and get some more. Maybe the groom won't show up before you get back."

They were wrong. The groom did come while the five foolish ones were gone, and the five who were ready went with the wedding party into the house. The door was locked behind them, and when the five who had not been prepared came running back they were too late to get in to the party. (*Matthew* 25:1-13)

Here's another illustration. "A rich man was going away for awhile, so he called his servants and turned over his property to them to manage. To the one he thought was most able to handle money he gave ten thousand dollars. To another he gave five thousand, and to another he gave a thousand.

"The one who got the ten thousand wasted no time in buying and selling until he had turned the original ten thousand into twenty thousand. The one who got the five thousand also put his money to good use, doubling it before the owner returned. But the one who had the smallest amount took it and hid it away.

"After a long absence, the rich man came back and called the three in to check on his money. The first one came with accounts showing that he had turned the ten thousand dollars into twenty thousand.

'That's the way to do business,' the owner complimented. 'You showed me that you can handle business well. I am going to put you in charge of bigger operations.'

"The second one got the same response. When he showed how he had parlayed the five thousand into ten thousand, the owner promised him more responsibility and more share in the estate. But with the third one, it was a different story.

"'Master, I knew you were a hard man, insisting on making a profit whatever the business deal, so I was afraid I might lose money for you. I hid the money away that you left with me. Here it is. You've got it all back safely.'

"The owner's answer was quick and sharp. 'You lazy scoundrel! If you knew that I insisted on making a profit, why didn't you at least put the money in the bank and let it draw interest for me? I'm giving your money to somebody that knows how to use it!' And he turned the thousand dollars over to the one who had made ten thousand.

"'Why should the one who had the most money get this too?' the question was put to the owner.'

"'Because in this life the person who has much and uses it wisely will be given more, and the person who doesn't use what he/she has will have even that taken away."

In addition to the obvious point in Matthew's story that not every person has the same amount of ability or possessions but every person must invest what she or he has in God's service, Luke's story adds another dimension. *Luke* has the rich man leaving for awhile to go and be appointed king by the ruling government. And some of the people he left at home actively campaigned against his appointment. What happens to those who work against the kingdom of God? In the end of the story they get wiped out. Don't oppose God's rule in life, and don't just sit on what you have.

Did the Pharisees then, and now, get the point that the real business of religion is not to keep all our understanding of the Way of God just as it has been passed along to us from the past, but to work at improving it? (*Matthew* 25:14-30; *Luke* 19:12-27)

Even the final judgment will be based not on what we know or profess, but on what we do. The most vivid picture Jesus drew of it fits the setting His people had heard about often. The Son of Man, or Messiah, is pictured as coming back to earth with a whole company of angels. He will sit on a great throne and all the people of the earth will parade before Him for judgment. They will be separated into two groups, much as a shepherd may separate sheep from goats in his herds, with the good people going to the Messiah's right side and the bad ones to His left. And the Messiah-King will say to those on His right hand, "Come, you fortunate ones, blessed by God; you now inherit the kingdom of God which was prepared for you from the beginning of God's plan.

"I was hungry, and you gave me food. I was thirsty and you gave me something to drink. I was a stranger, and you made me feel welcome. I was naked, and you clothed me. I was sick, and you came to visit me. I was in prison, and you visited me there too."

"What?" said the people to whom those words were addressed. "We never did any of those things. We never fed You when You were hungry, or gave You drink, or clothed You, or visited You when You were sick or in prison. When did we ever do that for You?"

"When you did any of those kind things for any person in need, you did it to me," the king replied. "But these people on my left are not fit to enter heaven. They are left to burn in the fires of their own selfishness and callousness." And turning to them, He said:

"I was hungry and you never fed me. I was thirsty and you didn't give me anything to drink. I was a stranger and you didn't welcome me, nor did you offer me clothes when I was naked. And when I was sick and in prison you never came to visit me."

"Wait a minute, Lord!" they exclaimed. "Just tell us when we ever saw You hungry, or thirsty, or naked, or a stranger, or sick, or in prison, and didn't do anything for You?"

"I tell you honestly, when you failed to do those acts of mercy to your fellow human beings in need, you failed to do them for Me."

That's the way the righteous will be divided from the ones who miss eternal life. (*Matthew* 25:31-46)

Keep your eyes open and you can learn about life even from people who are immoral themselves. Jesus told His disciples a story about some of them.

"There was a rich absentee landlord who left the operation of his farm to an overseer who was accused of mismanagement. The owner called for an accounting, and then fired the manager.

"'Now what am I going to do?' the former manager asked himself. 'I'm not strong enough for physical labor, and I'm ashamed to beg. I've got it! I'll put some people in a spot where they will have to support me.'

"So he called in the people with whom he had done business as steward of the rich man's farm. 'How much do you still owe my employer?' he asked one of them. 'I owe him for five hundred and fifty gallons of oil,' he replied.

"'Take your bill and write 275 gallons on it instead of 550.'

"Another one who owed five hundred bushels of wheat was instructed to change his bill to read 'eighty' and he did. Now the dishonest manager had something with which to blackmail them in the future.

"When he found out about it, the rich owner complimented the manager for being so cunning. And it is often true that unscrupulous persons are wiser at manipulating business deals than honest people are.

"Learn from the dishonest manager. He used material goods to provide a place for him to stay during his life here. You use material goods in such a way that those you have helped in this life will be friends for you in life beyond this one.

"The person who is a trustworthy steward of small amounts will also be trustworthy with large amounts. The person who is dishonest in small things can't be trusted with big things either. Being a steward of material possessions is a small matter compared with being a steward of true riches of human relationships. And if you can't handle honestly and wisely what somebody else entrusts to you, how can you handle real treasures of spiritual life that could be yours?

"No servant can serve two masters. Finally, he or she has to be devoted to only one. So you have to choose. Will you serve God, or money and the wealth of this world?"

Religous leaders who loved money scoffed at Jesus' emphasis as too 'other-worldly,' but Jesus told them 'You can go ahead and try to justify yourselves before people, but God knows your hearts. Material things so important to your crowd are worthless in God's sight.'" (*Luke* 16:1-15)

Every day that week He taught in the temple courtyard, and every night He went out of the city somewhere on the Mount Olivet side to spend the night. Each morning the crowds were in the temple early to hear what He had to say. (*Luke* 21:37-38)

The week was moving on, and just two days before the Passover Day, the chief priest and leading lawyers were trying desperately to think of some trick by which they could trap Jesus and have Him executed. It couldn't be on the day of the festival of Passover, they figured, or there might be a riot which would get out of hand. (*Matthew* 26:1-5; *Mark* 14:1-2; *Luke* 22:1-2)

On Thursday evening, while they were busy plotting, Jesus was in a Jerusalem suburb called Bethany eating supper at the house of Simon who had been a leper. Suddenly a woman came in with an alabaster bottle of very expensive perfume and startled everyone by breaking the neck of the bottle and pouring the perfume over Jesus' head. People gasped. Then some of them began to mutter:

"My! What a terrible waste of costly perfume! That much perfume would sell for hundreds of dollars, and she could have given that money to the poor."

But Jesus broke in, "Let her alone. Let's not make her feel uncomfortable, because what she has done for me is a very beautiful thing. You always have the poor with you, and you can show your love for them any time you want to, but you will not always have me with you. Actually, she has anointed my body for burial even before my death. She has done as much as she can do for me. I tell you that this deed of hers will never be forgotten. Wherever the Gospel is preached around the world, people will tell this story and remember her kindness." (*Matthew* 22:6-13; *Mark* 14:3-9)

Luke also has a story about Jesus' being anointed with costly perfume. But *Luke* 7:36-50 fits the incident into the ministry in Galilee, and the Simon of his story is a Pharisee instead of a leper. The woman is described as a sinner, and she broke the perfume bottle over His feet instead of His head, then she wet His feet with her tears and wiped them with her long hair as she kissed them.

The Pharisee wasn't concerned about the wasted money; He couldn't handle the fact that Jesus would let a woman like her touch Him. Jesus took the occasion to tell Simon a quick story and ask him a loaded question:

"A certain creditor had two people owing money. One owed five hundred dollars and the other fifty. When they couldn't pay, the creditor forgave them both. Now, which one do you think would appreciate the creditor more?"

"I'm sure the one who owed the five hundred would," Simon replied.

"You're right, of course," Jesus said. Then He turned toward the woman. "You see this woman? When I came into your house, you didn't give me any water to wash my feet, but she has wet them with her tears and wiped them with her hair. You gave me no kiss of greeting, but she hasn't stopped kissing my feet. You didn't anoint my head with oil, but she anointed my feet with this perfumed ointment. You know something? Her sins which were many are forgiven because she has loved much; but the person who has little to be forgiven loves only a little."

To the woman He then said gently, "Your sins are forgiven."

Others who were there at the meal had to question that, of course. "Who is this that says He forgives sins?"

Jesus still gave His attention to the woman. "Your faith has saved you from your old life. Now go in peace." He would rather help a person than argue theology.

To Golgotha and God

Sometime that day, Judas Iscariot slipped away from the other disciples and went to the chief priests with a proposition. For a price, he would see that Jesus fell into their hands. They arranged the deal, and all the rest of that day Judas watched for a good opportunity to betray Jesus, some place where the sympathetic crowd would not be around Him.

That afternoon some of His disciples asked, "Where do You want us to get a place for the Passover meal?"

Jesus gave them these instructions:

"Go into town and you will meet a man carrying a pitcher of water. Watch where he goes because I want you to speak to the master of the house he enters. Tell him 'The Master wants to know which room He will use to have the Passover meal with His disciples.' This man will show you a large upstairs room which will have everything in it we need. Make all the necessary preparations for the meal there."

So the two disciples He selected left for the city and found everything just as Jesus had predicted. They prepared for the Passover meal and waited there for Jesus and the others to come.

It was nighttime when Jesus arrived with the twelve. The meal began, and right in the middle of it Jesus threw in this remark which struck like a bombshell,

"One of you sitting right here at supper with me is going to turn against me tonight."

They couldn't believe it. Immediately they began to protest; each one of them was saying "I know I'm not the one."

But Jesus said it again, "Yes, it is one of the twelve—somebody who is eating with us right here, right now. The prophesy of the old scriptures will be fulfilled, but too bad for the man who actually betrays me to the authorities! He'd be better off if he had never been born."

Before the meal was over, Jesus took a small loaf of bread in His hands. He gave a prayer of thanksgiving, and then He broke it and gave some to each one of them.

"Take this bread and eat it. It is my body."

Then He picked up the cup, thanked God in a word of prayer, and passed the cup around to each of them as He said, "This is my blood which I must give in order that you may all be bound to God by a new bond. This is the last meal I will eat on this earth. I really wanted to eat it with you." (*Matthew* 25:14-29; *Mark* 14:10-25; *Luke* 22:3-20)

What a terrible time for some of the disciples to bring up the question again about who would be the greatest in the future order of things! But this is precisely where *Luke* adds the answers Jesus gave them, discussion which *Mark* reports in 10:42-45 and *Matthew* in 20:25-28.

"You know that the rulers of the gentile nations lord it over their people and expect to be called 'great.' But it shouldn't be that way among you. Whoever would be great among you must be the servant, and the leader must be one who serves most. I didn't come here to be served, did I? No, I came to serve, and to give my life for others. Before you are through following me you will be like judges to the twelve tribes of Israel, but your greatness must be measured in terms of service." (*Luke* 22:24-30)

"Now you are going to be on your own. You remember that I sent you out without any provisions and you didn't lack anything you really needed?"

"That's right," they admitted.

"But now," Jesus continued, "you will have to provide for yourselves, even for your own defense, because you will be treated as outlaws just as I am."

"Well, we have two swords here," somebody said.

"Enough of that," Jesus said as He began to sing one of the great old hymns. One by one they joined in, and all of them left the room singing. Jesus led them out of town again, along the side of the Mount of Olives. They were in deep thought as they walked along. They were all worried about Jesus' words to them, "Everyone of you will lose your faith in me before this is over. You remember the scripture 'the shepherd will be killed and the sheep scattered.' But after I have risen I will meet you again in Galilee!"

"Well, that may be true of the rest of them," Peter had said, "that they will lose faith in You, but I guarantee I'll never go back on You!"

And Jesus had replied, "Peter, I hate to say this, but before the rooster crows twice in the morning you will have sworn three times that you don't even know me."

"Why, Master, that is impossible!" Peter had come back. "Even if they kill me, they will never make me desert You."

And all the other disciples had said the same thing.

But then they came to a garden called Gethsemane on the side of the Mount of Olives. Jesus stopped and said, "You men find a place to sit down. I want to pray about this."

Taking Peter, James and John aside with Him, Jesus moved a little way from the rest of the group.

"I want you to be here praying for me," He told them, because I am facing a terrible ordeal, and my heart is breaking."

He went a few steps farther on and fell on the ground, praying in deep anguish, "My Father, everything is possible for You. If there is any other way, let me not have to take the way of the cross. Still, I want only to do what You want me to do—not what I want."

That was the way He prayed for a long time, with such intensity that His sweat was like big drops of blood. Then when He turned back to the three disciples, He found them lying on the ground sound asleep. It was Peter to whom He spoke:

"Simon, are you asleep here? Couldn't you stay awake and pray for a single hour? All of you had better be praying earnestly that you may not have to face this ordeal with me. Your intentions are good, but you don't realize how weak your human nature is."

But when He went aside again to continue praying, they couldn't keep their eyes open, and they were thoroughly ashamed when He caught them dozing once again.

"Are you still sleeping? Well, you had better wake up now because the time has come! You are going to see me fall into the hands of evil men. Look—here they come. See, my betrayer is here."

He had hardly finished speaking when Judas (one of the twelve disciples) stepped up out of the darkness to stand next to Jesus. Behind him was a big gang of men all armed with swords and clubs. Judas had arranged a signal, "Now the one I kiss on the cheek—He is the one you are after. Grab Him and carry Him off. I don't think He will give you any trouble."

There was a moment of strained silence. Then Judas said in a forced voice, "Good evening, Master," and leaned over and kissed Him with a show of affection.

The men leaped forward and pinned His arms. One of the disciples sprang to Jesus' defense; he struck out with his sword, slashing off the ear of the personal servant of the High Priest.

"Put your sword up!" Jesus ordered. "Everyone who takes the sword will perish by the sword. If I wanted to ask God for help now, I could have twelve legions of angels. But for now we must let the scriptures be fulfilled."

Then, without haste or excitement, Jesus spoke to the threatening gang:

"So, here you are, sneaking up here in the dead of the night to capture me as if I were a bandit! All day, every day, I have stood right in the temple teaching. Yet you never laid a finger on me. But of course, this fulfills the scriptures."

When His disciples realized that He was not going to resist, they went over the garden wall to escape into the darkness. One boy who had gone with them to the garden was grabbed as he started to run; but he wrenched himself loose, leaving his long linen shirt in the hands of the soldier and escaped into the night stark naked. (*Mark* 14:26-50; *Matthew* 26:30-56; *Luke* 22:21-53)

The armed mob surrounded Jesus and pushed Him along into the city where the High Priest and all the chief priests and elders were waiting. They didn't notice that Simon Peter followed them all the way, keeping them in sight but not getting close enough to be recognized. Peter slipped into the High Priest's courtyard and got into a group of servants who were warming themselves by a fire. (*Mark* 14:53-54; *Matthew* 26:58)

Inside Caiphas' house the "witnesses" against Jesus were all ready to tell their lies. The midnight session of the court, the chief priests and the council, had to find some "evidence" against Jesus that would make it seem that He deserved the death penalty.

The witnesses couldn't agree on their stories. Some said, "We heard Him say that He would destroy this temple which was built by men, and in three days He would build another one without any human help."

They wanted to prove that Jesus was claiming to be God, which was blasphemy—the most serious crime of all for the Jews.

Finally the High Priest himself stood up and stepped out into the middle of the floor where Jesus stood quietly.

"Can't you make any answer?" he asked Jesus. "What are you going to say about all this evidence against you?"

But Jesus never said a word.

Again the High Priest asked Him, "Are you the Christ, the Son of God?"

Then Jesus answered him, "I am! And there will be a day when you see the Son of Man sitting at God's right hand, coming in the clouds from heaven."

The High Priest sprang back from Him, tearing his clothes, yelling excitedly:

"You heard Him. All of you heard Him. It's blasphemy. Do we still need witnesses? What shall we do with Him?"

"He must die," they cried out. Some of them spit on Him and some of them put a blindfold on Him. Then they stood around Him hitting Jesus hard and taunting Him:

"Now prophesy who hit you!"

Even the servants who were ordered to take charge of Him slapped His face and abused Him.

Meanwhile, Peter was down in the courtyard below. One of the High Priest's maids noticed him standing by the fire. Somehow she thought she recognized him. She kept staring at his face in the flickering firelight and suddenly exclaimed,

"Why, you were one of the men who followed this Jesus of Nazareth!"

"What are you talking about? I don't even know Him," Peter asserted. Nervously he moved away from the firelight and edged toward the gate. Somewhere a rooster crowed.

But the maid was still convinced that she had seen him. She repeated in a positive voice to the men standing there, "He is one of them all right."

Again Peter denied it. Now some of the men were suspicious too.

"Yes, you do look like one of them, and your speech is Galilean!"

"Listen," Peter snarled, "I swear I don't even know this man you are talking about!"

He hardly had the words out of his mouth before the rooster crowed a second time in the darkness before dawn. (Just then, *Luke* adds, they were bringing Jesus back across the courtyard and Jesus turned to look Peter straight in the eye.) And suddenly Peter remembered what Jesus had said to him in the Garden of Gethsemane,

"Before the rooster crows twice, you will have sworn three times that you don't even know me."

As he slipped out of the gate, Peter broke down. Great sobs shook his body as he wept alone in the early dawn. (*Mark* 14:55-72; *Matthew* 26:59-75; *Luke* 22:56-71)

Daylight came and the chief priests called the rest of the council to meet together. After a brief consultation they ordered Jesus taken in shackles to the Roman governor, Pontius Pilate.

The governor was interested in one thing only: Was Jesus a dangerous leader who might cause a revolt against the government? So this is the question he asked Jesus as soon as He was brought before him:

"Are you the king of the Jews?"

And Jesus answered, "You have said so."

Then the chief priests began listing all their reasons for bringing Jesus to ask the death penalty for Him.

"Don't you have anything to say in your defense?" Pilate asked Jesus. "You hear all the accusations they are making about you."

Jesus just stood absolutely silent, so Pilate didn't know what to make of it. (*Mark* 15:1-5; *Matthew* 27:1-2, 11-14; *Luke* 22:66; 23:1-3)

Finally, Pilate turned to the chief priests and their followers.

"I find nothing with which to charge this man," he told them bluntly.

"What about inciting people to rebellion against Rome?" they called back. "This man has been stirring up the people with His teaching all through the country, from Galilee to Jerusalem."

As soon as Pilate heard that, he knew he had a way out of his dilemma. "You say this man is a Galilean? It just happens that Herod is in town. He belongs in Herod's jurisdiction. Take him to Herod."

Herod was more than glad to see Jesus. He had heard so much about Jesus, and he hoped to persuade Jesus to perform some miracles for him. It should be quite a show, he figured.

They brought Jesus in to him, and Herod had several questions to ask. But Jesus never made any reply at all. His silence agitated the accusing priests and lawyers even more. They shouted all kinds of accusations, and even Herod and his men made fun of Jesus with their insults. When they tired of that, they dressed Him in a kingly robe and sent Him back to the Roman governor. Until this time, Pilate and Herod had been bitter enemies, but their common mistreatment of Jesus opened communication between them and they became friends.

Pilate still would not change his opinion in the case.

"Listen," he laid it out to the priests and the people who side with them, "you brought this man before me once, and I examined him and told you that I did not find him to be guilty of any of the charges you made against him. Now Herod has sent him back to me. Obviously he couldn't find anything deserving death either. So I am going to have him whipped and released." (*Luke* 23:4-16)

But the religious leaders weren't through yet. They knew that every year since he had been governor Pilate had let the Jews pick one prisoner, anybody they chose, at the Passover Festival time, and the Romans would free that person.

"What about your custom of letting us have a prisoner freed? Let us choose one."

"Do you want me to give freedom to the 'King of the Jews?' the governor asked. He knew very well that the chief priests had handed Jesus over to him out of sheer hatred. And he was wondering just how seriously he should take the message from his wife, delivered only a few moments before, "Don't have anything to do with this righteous man. I am very disturbed by a dream I had about Him."

Pilate was not surprised when their stooges in the crowd began to shout,

"No, we want Barabbas instead!"

Barabbas was a riot leader who had committed murder in a recent revolt which the Romans had quickly put down. "We want Barabbas. We want Barabbas!"

Then what do you want me to do with the man who is called the "King of the Jews?" Pilate asked the crowd.

And the horrifying answer came back:

"Crucify him!"

Pilate tried to reason with them. The shouts rose to a frenzied roar,

"Crucify him! Crucify him!"

And Pilate gave in. He wanted to satisfy the ugly crowd for fear it might get out of hand, so he ordered that Barabbas be released. Then he took a basin of water and washed his hands in their sight, saying "I am innocent of this man's blood. But because of your insistence I am going to have him flogged and crucified." (*Mark* 15:6-15; *Matthew* 27:15-26; *Luke* 23:17-25)

It was cruel sport for the hardened soldiers. After the public whipping, they dragged Him into the courtyard of the Roman headquarters and called every man of the battalion to assemble for the show. One of them brought a purple robe and they put it on Jesus. Then they twisted some thorn branches into a crown and jammed it down on His head. Meanwhile, they shouted with mockery in their voices,

"Hail, your majesty! King of the Jews!"

While they yelled their taunts, they hit Him on the head with a stick and they spit on Him. Some of them bowed down before Him, making fun of the "royal majesty" they had conferred on Him.

Finally, they got tired of their "fun." They took off the purple cloak, put His own clothes on Him again, and led Him outside the government buildings to take Him to the place outside the city walls for execution on a cross. Before they had gone very far they grabbed a man named Simon, who was the father of Alexander and Rufus, and made him carry the beam for Jesus' cross. Simon was a native of Cyrene in Africa and just happened to be passing by at the time. (*Mark* 15:16-21; *Matthew* 27:27-32)

A great crowd of people followed through the narrow street, including women who wept loudly in anguish and protest over His treatment. Once Jesus turned to them and said "Daughters of Jerusalem, don't weep for me, but weep for yourselves and your children. The days are coming when the women who never got to be mothers will be most fortunate. People will be saying to the mountains, 'Fall on us; cover us up,' as they try to find some safe place to hide. If they do this to one who is innocent of rebellion, what will they do to those who are guilty when that day comes?''

Two other men, condemned as criminals, were also being led in the procession to be put to death alongside Jesus. (*Luke* 23:26-32)

Up the hill of Golgotha, which means ''the place of the skull,'' they made their way. Before they put Him on the cross, they offered Him some drugged wine prepared by the women of Jerusalem to ease the pain, but Jesus refused to drink it. Then they stretched Him out on the cross timbers and drove nails through His hands into the wood and left Him hanging there in agony. Over His head they hung a sign, the way they announced the crime for which the crucified was being punished. Jesus' inscription read ''THE KING OF THE JEWS.''

At the foot of His cross, the soldiers sorted out His clothes and drew lots to see what each one of them would get. It was about nine o'clock in the morning now.

The two robbers were being crucified at the same time, one on each side of Jesus.

Now everybody joined in mocking Him. Onlookers in the crowd wagged their heads and shouted,

''Hey, you, didn't you say you would destroy the temple and build it again in three days? Well, why don't you come down from your cross and save yourself? That ought to be an even easier trick!''

The priests and the scribes thought they were being funny in saying to each other, ''He came to 'save' others; why, He can't even save Himself. Now if He really wanted us to believe in Him as the Messiah, the

King of Israel, He would come down from His cross. Then we would believe it." (*Mark* 15:22-32; *Matthew* 27:33-43; *Luke* 23:33-35)

Still continuing their cruel fun, the soldiers joined in mocking Him.

"Here, have a drink!" they said as they offered Him vinegar. "You hear what they are saying; if you are the King of the Jews, save yourself!"

Even one of the other men on a nearby cross added his taunt, "Aren't you the Messiah? Save yourself, and save us too!"

But the man on the third cross rebuked the one who had flung that jibe at Jesus, "Don't you even fear God? We are all in this together. And we deserve the sentence passed on us because we are guilty, but this man has done nothing wrong."

Then, looking at Jesus he added, "Jesus, remember me when You come into Your kingdom."

"Don't worry, my friend," Jesus replied. "Today you will be with me in Paradise." (*Luke* 23:36-43)

Noontime came after three long hours of torture, and a strange darkness settled over the land. Hanging on the cross there in the fearful gloom, Jesus continued to suffer as the minutes crawled by. The fourth hour passed, then the fifth, and the sixth—until finally at three o'clock Jesus cried out, "My God, my God, why have You forsaken me?"[1]

When some of the people heard these words spoken by Jesus (Eli, Eli, lama sabachthani), they misunderstood Him.

"Did you hear that? He's calling for Elijah!"

One man in the crowd dipped a sponge in some

[1] *Psalm* 22 begins with these words of utter despair but ends on a note of complete confidence in God's final victory. Was Jesus thinking of this?

vinegar, fixed it to the end of a stick and held it up for Jesus to suck. He said to the others, "Let's watch now and see if Elijah will come and take Him down!"

But Jesus gave one more loud cry and died after breathing one last prayer,

"Father, into Your hands I commend my spirit!"[2]

At that same moment, the curtain in the temple which kept the "holy of holies" from the sight of ordinary people was split in two from top to bottom. (*Mark* 15:33-38; *Matthew* 27:45-51a; *Luke* 23:44-46)

Matthew adds that "there was an earthquake which split rocks in two, opened graves and some of the saints were resurrected and seen by many people in Jerusalem. (27:51-53)

The Roman centurion in charge of the crucifixion stood in wonder in front of Jesus' cross. He had watched Jesus carefully all the time, and when He died the centurion said aloud,

"He must surely have been a Son of God!"

And many of the onlookers went home that day overcome with remorse.

All this time some of the women who followed Jesus had been waiting at a distance. Mary of Magdala, Mary, the mother of the younger James and of Joses, the mother of the disciples, James and John, and Salome were among them. This group of women had been faithful companions of His up in Galilee and had always been ready to look after His needs. They had not deserted Him in the last hours. (*Mark* 15:39-41; *Matthew* 27:54-56; *Luke* 23:47-49)

As soon as Jesus died, Joseph of Arithmathea, one member of the Jewish National Council who believed in the kingdom of God which Jesus preached, went

[2] This is little bedtime prayer every Jewish child learned at home.

directly to Pilate and asked him to let him take the body of Jesus for burial. He had to move fast in order to get the burial finished before the Sabbath began at sunset. Pilate was surprised that Jesus was reported dead so soon, so he sent a messenger to check with the centurion to make sure. When the centurion's word came back, Pilate gave Joseph his approval for taking the body of Jesus.

Joseph bought a long linen cloth and hurried back to the execution ground. As gently as he could, he took Jesus from the cross and wrapped him in the winding sheet. Not too far away there was a tomb that had been carved from the solid rock for Him, so Joseph had the body laid there. He had a huge stone rolled in front of the entrance to close it up tight.

All the while, Mary of Magdala and Mary, the mother of Joses, were watching to see exactly where Jesus was being buried. Then they went back into the city and waited all the next day until the Sabbath was over at sundown. That evening they hurried out to buy spices and ointment to prepare the body properly for permanent burial. (*Mark* 15:42-47; *Matthew* 27:57-61; *Luke* 23:50-56)

The next day some of the Jewish leaders went to Pilate with a request.

"Sir, we remember how that imposter, Jesus, said that He would rise from the tomb after three days. If you will just order the tomb to be made secure through the third day, His disciples won't have a chance to steal the body away and tell everybody that He has risen from the dead. If they arrange to do that, the last fraud will be worse than the first."

"You have a guard of soldiers," Pilate told them. "You go and make it as secure as you can."

Secure it they did. They sealed the large stone at the entrance and also placed an armed guard to watch it. (*Matthew* 27:62-66)

Very early on Sunday morning, just as the sun was rising, the women arrived at the tomb. On the way they had worried about one thing: who would roll away the heavy stone at the entrance? Much to their surprise, they saw that the stone had already been rolled back. (*Matthew* explains that an angel had done it with the force of an earthquake. And the official guards were so frightened at seeing the dazzling appearance of the angel that they were immobilized.) Cautiously the women looked inside but there was no body there. Instead they saw either one (*Mark* and *Matthew*) or two (*Luke*) angels like young men sitting in the tomb.

"Don't be afraid," they heard the angel voice say. "You are looking for Jesus who was crucified, but He is not here. He has risen as He said He would! Look, here is the place His body was laid. Remember how He told you in Galilee that He had to be delivered up to sinful men who would crucify Him, but that on the third day He would rise?"

They remembered, of course.

"But don't stay here," the angel speaker continued, "go and tell His disciples and Peter that He will meet them in Galilee just as He said He would."

The women hurried away from the tomb, trembling with excitement. They just couldn't believe their eyes and ears, so they didn't dare say a word about it to anyone, *Mark* says. Both *Matthew* and *Luke* say they ran to tell the others. (*Mark* 16:1-8; *Matthew* 28:1-8; *Luke* 24:1-9)

Although there were several women, including Mary of Magdala, Joanna and Mary, the mother of James, all in agreement on the story, the men would not believe them. But curiosity got the better of Peter. He left the group and ran to the tomb, looked inside and saw the linen grave cloths lying by themselves, and then went back trying to figure out what had happened. (*Luke* 24:10-12)

Matthew says that Jesus Himself met the women as they turned to go back into the city. He stood there while they fell at His feet to worship Him. And He also reassured them, "Don't be afraid. Go tell my companions to go to Galilee, and they will see me there." (*Matthew* 28:9-10)

Now the resurrection appearance stories tumble out of the three Gospels in a way that almost seems to defy arranging them by time and place. Evidently some people said the living Christ was one place while others said His appearances were in other locales. In accepting all the Gospel accounts as part of the story of Jesus, the Church did not insist on conformity of the reports. After all, He might now be anywhere anytime, or everywhere all the time!

Some early copies of *Mark* have no additional verses after 16:8, but other early manuscripts continue the story this way:

"Mary of Magdala was the first person to whom the risen Jesus appeared. She went to the place where His other disciples were grieving and told them that He was alive and that she had seen Him; but they would not believe her story.

Later on, as two of the disciples were walking along a road outside the city, they saw Him too, and they hurried back to Jerusalem to tell the others about it. Still the group would not believe it.

Still later, He appeared to the eleven themselves as they were eating a meal together and made them feel sorry for their lack of faith since they hadn't believed the ones who had seen Him. Then He told them,

"You must go all over the world and tell the good news to everyone. The person who believes you and is baptized will be saved, but the person who does not believe you will be lost. There will be special things the believers can do: they will heal people in

My name; they will talk a new language; they will be able to pick up snakes and even will be able to withstand poison."

"After this final appearance to His disciples, Jesus was taken up into heaven to be with God. His disciples went out and began to preach everywhere. The risen Lord worked with them and they were able to do all these special things as He had promised." (*Mark* 16:9-20)

Matthew is the one that included the story of guards being set up to watch the tomb by Jewish religious leaders who didn't want to take a chance that the body of Jesus would be stolen and a "resurrection" story circulated by Jesus' disciples. So Matthew adds this ending to the story of the guards who simply stood by amazed as the women discovered the empty tomb, heard the angel's words, and then ran back to tell the other disciples:

"While the women were going, part of the tomb guard force went immediately to tell the chief priests what had taken place. Their story caused a hasty summoning of several elders, and all together they decided to give the soldiers money to tell people that His disciples came at night and took the body away while we were asleep. 'And if the governor hears about this, we will satisfy him and keep you out of trouble.' The soldiers took the money and began spreading that story which is still being circulated today."

Following that item, *Matthew* simply adds a concluding paragraph which says,

"The eleven disciples did go to Galilee, to a mountain Jesus had suggested as a meeting place. There they saw Him and worshipped Him, but even then some doubted." And what were the final words of Jesus to them, and to the Church for whom the Gospel was written?

"All authority in heaven and on earth has been given Me," Jesus told them. "So you go now and make disciples of all the people of all the nations, baptizing them in the name of the Father and Son and Holy Spirit. Teach them everything that I have commanded you, and you will discover that I am with you always, even to the close of the age." (*Matthew* 28:11-20)

That's it. But *Luke* had collected other stories which he couldn't leave out of his account. After saying that the disciples inside the city couldn't believe the story brought to them from the tomb by the women, he tells about a Sunday walk of two of the group who were going from Jerusalem to the town of Emmaus, about seven miles from the city. They were talking with each other about all the things that had happened recently. While they were moving along Jesus Himself joined them and walked along with them. Neither of them recognized Him.

"What is it that you are talking about so earnestly as you are walking along?" Jesus asked.

They both stopped dead still, sadness written all over their faces. Then one of them, Cleopas, answered, "Are you the only visitor to Jerusalem who doesn't know what has happened there in the last few days?"

"What things?" Jesus asked innocently.

"Everything concerning Jesus of Nazareth," they answered. "He was a great prophet both in word and deed before God and all the people. Our own chief priests and rulers gave Him to the Romans to be condemned to death. And they crucified Him. We had hoped that He was the Messiah Who would redeem Israel. But that's not all. This is the third day since He was killed, and this morning some women of our group told us an amazing story. Very early this morning they were at the tomb where He was buried, but they did not find any body. They came back to us saying that they had seen angels who told them that Jesus is still alive. Some of our group went out to the tomb to check their story, and they couldn't find the body either."

"Is that so unbelievable?" Jesus asked. "Why should you be so slow to believe all the prophets have spoken? Wasn't it necessary that the Messiah should suffer all these things and then enter His glory?"

Never had they listened so intently as they now listened as this unknown companion explained to them all the references of Scripture to the Messiah. He began with Moses and told the whole story.

By then they were close to the village of Emmaus. Jesus acted as if He were going to pass through and travel on, but they insisted that He stay overnight with them. "It's too late for you to walk farther. We would really like it if you would stay overnight with us."

Then, at the supper table, it happened. The guest took the bread and broke the loaf as He blessed it. Now they recognized Him. Then He was gone. They looked at each other as the realization washed over them: "Didn't our hearts burn within us when He was talking to us on the road? We should have known when He opened the meaning of the scriptures to us!"

No longer were they hungry or tired. Daylight or darkness made no difference; they couldn't wait to get back to Jerusalem and tell the others. Straight to the place where the inner group of disciples were gathered they hurried.

"Have we got news for you!" they said to the ones closest to the door.

"First, we have something to tell you," the response came. "Since you were here, the Lord has appeared to Peter. He really has risen."

"We know it too," they cut in. "We saw Him also." And they told what had happened on the road, and how they finally knew Him as He broke the bread at their table. As they were telling their story, Jesus suddenly appeared right there with them. Most of them reacted as if they were seeing a ghost. Startled and frightened, they heard the familiar word "Shalom." And then He asked them, "Why are you frightened? Look at me. Look at my hands and feet. Touch me if you want. A ghost doesn't have flesh and bones, does it?"

Still they couldn't believe what they were seeing and hearing, but the fear was being replaced in their minds by a sense of joy that seemed unreasonable as well. So Jesus continued to demonstrate His real Presence. "Do you have anything to eat around here?"

Somebody handed Him a piece of broiled fish, and while they were watching closely He ate it. Then He followed that up by saying, "You know I told you while I was with you that everything written in the entire scripture about Me had to be fulfilled." And He did for the whole group what He had done for the two on the road to Emmaus; He reviewed all the writings which emphasized that the Messiah had to suffer and be killed and then rise on the third day from the dead.

"Now you are to become part of that story. In the Messiah's name, you are to preach the Good News that all people may repent and be forgiven by God for their sins. Start right here where you are in Jerusalem. You are the witnesses to all these things, but first stay here together until you are filled with the power of God which I promised you."

Once again they made the trek from the meeting room in the city down across the Kidron valley and around the side of the Mount of Olives, with Jesus leading just as He had the night He was taken by the soldiers. This time they passed the Garden of Gethsemane and went farther up the road to Bethany. There He gave them a final blessing and then left them all as He had left the supper table in Emmaus.

Back to Jerusalem they went filled with joy. No longer did they hide in their rooms. In full view of everybody, including the authorities, they praised God in the temple every day, telling the Gospel story first in Jerusalem.

Next, the world! (*Luke* 24:13-53)

JOHN

THE SETTING

They say that a good speech has three parts:

You tell them what you are going to tell them,
You tell them,
And you tell them what you told them.

The writer of the Gospel of *John* follows that advice. He has a confident faith he wants to make perfectly clear.

There is only one way Human Beings can see and understand God. There is only one way Human Beings can find The Way through the darkness of this world to Eternal Life. The light for H.B.'s path must come from the Creator of life, but H.B. can only understand God in terms of human experience.

That perfect picture of God in a human life has come to us. The light of the world is Jesus of Nazareth, the long-awaited Messiah.

The Gospel of *John* uses incidents and conversation from the life of Jesus to illustrate why every reader should share this faith upon which the Church was being built around the Greco-Roman world as the second century A.D. was approaching.

JOHN'S INTRODUCTION

You have read the story of Jesus of Nazareth, but did you ever understand the meaning of it all? The story really begins in the very beginning of all creation. That creative part of God that brought all the created cosmos into being filled everything with life. That life is the source of intelligence and understanding in Human Beings. No matter how much darkness and ignorance there may seem to be, the light of God's life and truth is always present.

One who testified to that light was a man named John. He was not himself the Light personified, but was a witness sent from God to tell about the person who was the embodiment of the very Mind of God. That One came into the world, and though human life owed its being to Him, human beings did not recognize Him. He came as a human being but His own would not receive Him as the essence of God. But to everyone who did receive Him and accept His leadership, He opened to them the way to become children of God, no longer just children of human beings but true spirit children of God's own Self.

In other words, in this Human Being the creative Mind of God came to live with us human beings. We saw His spiritual fullness, saw it in Him in a unique and special way. He was full of the love of God and full of God's truth.

This is what John said about Him: "He is coming after me, but He is way ahead of me. Before I was born, He already lived."

Now we have the full gift of God for our life. The Law was given through Moses; now love and understanding have come through this Man, Jesus Christ. Nobody has ever seen God, of course; but this Son of God, dearest to God's heart, has made God known to us. (1:1-18)

THE STORY OF JESUS...

begins with the preaching of John the Baptist.

One day a delegation of priests and Levites were sent from headquarters in Jerusalem to the east side of the Jordan valley near Bethany where John was preaching and baptizing people. They wanted to find out who he was. Was he the Messiah the Jews were expecting?

"No, I am not," John answered them candidly.

"What are you, then?" they asked. "Are you Elijah?"

"No."

"Are you the special prophet Moses said we should look for?"

"Again, no."

"Then who are you? We have to give some answer to those who sent us!"

"I am carrying out the words of Isaiah: I am a voice crying in the wilderness, 'Make the highway straight for the Lord, get ready for the coming of the king.'"

"Well, if you aren't the Messiah, nor Elijah, and not the Prophet, why are you baptizing people?"

"I am baptizing with water; that's true," John said, "but there is One among you already, though you don't know Him, Who is the One for Whom I am preparing the way. I am not fit to be the slave that unties His shoes."

The next day John saw Jesus coming toward him.

"Look," John said suddenly to the people standing around him, "there He is, the One I have been telling you about, the One Who can take away the sins of the world! I didn't know Who it would be, but I have been here preaching repentance and calling for baptism in order to get Israel ready for Him to be revealed.

"I can see the Spirit of God coming down from heaven to rest on Him just as God let me know I would. Now I know that this is God's Chosen One Who will baptize people in God's Spirit!"

It was on the following day that John was standing with two of his disciples when Jesus passed by.

"There is the Lamb of God," John said, and the two

left John to try to catch up with Jesus. Jesus saw them following Him and stopped for them to catch up.

"What do you want?" Jesus asked them directly.

"Teacher, where are You staying?" one of them asked in return.

"Why don't you come and see?"

They did. They spent the rest of the day with Him, and the first thing that one of them, Andrew, did after leaving Jesus was to go find his brother Simon Peter.

"We have found the Messiah!" Andrew told Simon. "Come on, I'll introduce you." And the two hurried back to where Jesus was staying. When they met, Jesus looked steadily into Simon's face and then said quietly "You are Simon, son of John, now, but you shall be called Peter, or Cephas (the Rock)."

Accompanied by the two brothers, Jesus went north into Galilee. Somewhere they met Philip, who came from Bethsaida which was also the hometown of Andrew and Peter, a prominent city on the banks of the Jordan where it flows into the north end of the Lake of Galilee. Jesus invited Philip to join them, and Philip went to find his brother, Nathanael.

"We have met the man Moses and the prophets talked about," Philip told him excitedly. "He is Jesus, son of Joseph, from Nazareth."

"Nazareth! Can anything good come out of Nazareth?" Nathanael retorted.

"Just come and see," Philip answered.

When Jesus saw Nathanael coming back with Philip, He said out loud, "Now here is an Israelite worthy of the name; there is nothing devious about him."

Nathanael overheard and said, "How do You know anything about me?"

"I saw you under the fig tree before Philip found you," Jesus answered.

Captivated by the Person he saw before him,

Nathanael said what he was thinking. "Teacher, You are the Son of God; the anointed One of Israel!"

Smiling, Jesus answered, "Are you saying that just because I said that I saw you under the fig tree where you meditate and pray for the coming Kingdom? Well, you are going to see great things. You will have the vision of Israel himself, the heavens opening with God's angels going up and down. I will be the ladder for you." (1:19- 51)

Jesus brings fullness and zest to life. Right at the beginning of His ministry that fact was illustrated by an incident in Cana, a few miles north of Jesus' hometown of Nazareth. Jesus and His disciples had been invited to a wedding where His mother, Mary, was helping with arrangements for dinner.

A small crisis developed when the wine was all gone. The party had dragged on and Mary was embarrassed because the drink had given out.

"Can't you help us," she appealed to her son.

"I don't think the time has come for me to reveal who I am," Jesus replied.

Ignoring His remark, Mary showed her complete confidence in Him by telling the servants, "Do whatever He tells you to do."

In answer to their expectant gaze, Jesus looked around the room and noticed six large water jars set along one wall. They were the kind of containers used for religious ceremonies of purification in the temple. Here was a chance for the incomplete (6 instead of the perfect number 7 jars) gift of the Jewish Law to be made complete by the free grace of God's love.

"Fill these jars with water," Jesus instructed the servants. And they did—with about 150 gallons! (God's love is always more than enough to fill us!)"

"Now take pitchersfull out of the jars," Jesus ordered, "and take them to the man in charge." Noting that a new supply of wine had been brought in, the headwaiter tasted it to check its quality.

"What's this?" he asked the groom in genuine surprise. "Everybody serves the best wine first at parties like this, and when the guests have had a lot to drink he brings out a poorer brand. But this wine is even better than the drink you served at first!"

This was just the beginning of a long line of revealing acts of Jesus that led His disciples to be certain that He brought a completeness of joy to life which the old law could never match. (2:1-11)

Mary and Jesus' other brothers, along with the disciples of Jesus, went back to Capernaum with Him but they didn't have much time together there. Jesus was anxious to go on to Jerusalem to celebrate the Passover. What He found there shocked Him.

In the great temple, moneychangers had set up their tables where they charged a heavy commission for every coin they exchanged for regular currency many pilgrims brought with them. Temple authorities had ruled that only Jewish coins would be acceptable as payment of the temple tax which was required each year from every male Jew. Alongside the moneychangers' tables were cages of pigeons and doves, with smelly stalls full of cattle and sheep filling other parts of the temple area which was supposed to be set aside for the worship and prayer by non-Jewish visitors. Official "inspectors" made sure that birds and animals pilgrims may have brought with them were somehow "blemished" and not acceptable for temple sacrifice. The acceptable ones, peddled by the temple merchants, sold at exhorbitant prices.

"Get this unholy business out of here," Jesus shouted as he began turning over the moneychangers' tables. And while they were scrambling to retrieve their coins, He turned on the pigeon and dove merchants.

"Out! Take these cages away! You can't turn God's

House into a marketplace!''

And before they knew what was happening, Jesus added to the uproar by making whips of cords and stampeding the cattle and sheep out of the temple.

''Nothing can stop Him,'' the Galilean companions of Jesus said to each other. ''The old scripture said that God's anointed One would be filled with zeal for God's House.''

Now the religious keepers of the temple rallied to confront Him.

''Where do you think you get the authority to do what you are doing?'' they demanded. ''Just show us some sign from God—if you can—that you have divine authority!''

''Destroy this temple,'' Jesus challenged them, ''and in three days I will raise it up again.''

That answer left them sputtering in amazement. Not realizing that Jesus was referring to His own resurrection after being killed by them once they were in control of the situation, they took His reference to the temple literally.

''Why, it has taken forty-six years to build this temple (and it would be another twenty years before Herod's temple was completed). Forty-six years—and you could raise it again in three days?''

Even His disciples didn't understand His reference until after the resurrection. Then they saw how their scripture actually applied to everything Jesus was saying and doing. (2:12-22)

A good many other people came to be His followers while He was in Jerusalem for that Passover season because of all the wonderful and courageous things He did, but Jesus would not allow them to proclaim Him as the Messiah who would lead their fight for independence from Rome. He knew all too well how unstable would be their commitment to Him if it were based only on the sensational acts they had witnessed.

No one had to tell Jesus what the emotions and character of people were like. (2:23-25)

Even among religious leaders who were part of the Jewish Establishment, Jesus was having an unsettling effect. One Pharisee, Nicodemus, a member of the Sanhedrin, the highest Jewish Council, went to talk with Jesus one night while He was in Jerusalem.

His opening remarks to Jesus reveal the kind of interest Jesus was stirring.

"Teacher, everybody knows that You are a representative of God because nobody can do the things You have been doing if God is not with Him."

"It takes more than just recognizing the truth," Jesus said. "Unless a person is born anew, that person can never understand the kingdom of God."

"I guess I don't understand what You are saying," Nicodemus came back. "How is it possible for a person to be born again? You don't mean this literally, that a grown man could be born from his mother's womb again?"

"Of course not," Jesus picked up the statement again. "I am saying that two kinds of birth are necessary before a person becomes part of the true family of God. A person must be born physically, but a person must also be born spiritually. Only spirit can give birth to the spirit, just as flesh alone can produce a physical birth. Surely that idea doesn't astonish you. Since our word for "spirit" is also the word for "wind," take the wind as an illustration of what we mean here. You don't know where the wind comes from or where it goes, but you can see the effects of it and you know it has blown around us. The spirit of God is exactly the same. You may not know how to explain it, but you can tell when it is giving life to a person."

"Well, how is that possible?" Nicodemus asked, falling back on the customary theological debate approach.

"Look," Jesus answered, "I am not trying to talk in philosophical terms. Can't an educated teacher like you understand something this natural and common? If you can't see a plain, simple truth like this, how can we talk about deeper meanings of God's Kingdom? (3:1-12)

"Make sure of one thing," *John* now urges every reader (verses 13-15), "Jesus came directly from God to tell us the truths of God. Nobody else can do that. That is why people's attention must be directed to Him, as people looked at the bronze serpent Moses held up in the wilderness so they would have faith in God and be healed of the plague. (*Numbers* 21:4-9) Everyone who looks to Jesus and believes in God Whom He reveals will have this spirit of life which is eternal."

The manuscript attributes these statements to Jesus Himself. Either way, this message is the same heart of the Gospel:

"God loved the human world so much that God gave us Jesus so that everyone who is born in His Spirit will have Life that never ends. God did not send Him into the world to condemn human beings, but to be the means for saving them. Anyone who believes in Jesus and grows in His Spirit can be sure of being acceptable to God, but those who do not accept His authority already bring judgment on themselves. The reason is simple: the light has come into the world and they preferred darkness because they did not want their deeds and their character to be exposed to the light. They know that the light of God will show up their evil. On the other hand, people who have nothing to hide and want to do God's will in everything, welcome the light and come to live in it!" (3:16-21)

BEFORE HIS IMPRISONMENT... by Herod, John was still preaching and baptizing in the Jordan River area northeast of Judea, while Jesus and His disciples worked in Judea doing the same. There were still many people going out to be baptized by John, and John's disciples were constantly in a running argument with many Jewish leaders about how John's baptism fit into the Jewish scheme of purification. Now they had one more concern. "What should we think about the man you pointed out by the river one day? He is baptizing also, and crowds are flocking to Him instead of you."

Many public figures would have felt some jealousy in such a situation, but John kept his honest perspective. "We each one have what God gives us. You remember that I said then that I am only a forerunner of the Messiah; I am not the Messiah Himself. Jesus is like the bridegroom at the wedding; I am the best man standing by to do whatever I can to help. I am perfectly happy now that His public acceptance is increasing, and I am willing for mine to give way to His."

To which I can only add, the Gospel writer continues, that this is what I am saying: Jesus, Who comes from heaven, is Number One. Even great human teachers are bound to talk only from human experience, but the One Who comes from heaven can tell us what He has seen and heard. And still people do not accept His witness. He speaks God's truth because God has given Him the authority to do so; people who believe Him are saying 'Yes' to God. Put your faith in Jesus and you will have a hold on Eternal Life. If you won't line up with Jesus you will lose out because you will be going against God's Way. (3:22-36)

The news that Jesus and His disciples were baptizing more people than John had also come to the attention of the religious leaders in Jerusalem. Actually it was the disciples who were doing the baptizing, but Jesus knew that His popular movement was upsetting the establishment in Judea, so He decided to go north to Galilee. The shortest way was through Samaria, though most orthodox Jews would have traveled east to cross the Jordan, then north on the far side of the river in order to avoid any contact with Samaritans. By noon of the first day in Samaria Jesus and His group of followers had made it to a town called Sychar which was famous for having a deep well called "Jacob's well" just outside it on the plot of ground Jacob had given to his son Joseph and where Joseph's bones were buried. Tired from the journey, Jesus sat down by the well to rest.

Some of the disciples went on into town to get supplies, so they were not with Jesus when a woman came to the well to draw water.

"Would you be so kind as to give me a drink?" Jesus asked her.

"What!" the woman jerked around in surprise. "You ask me, a Samaritan woman, for a drink?" She knew that Jews and Samaritans wouldn't use the same cup or dipper. Ignoring her surprise that He would break such an unwritten law, Jesus returned this comment:

"If you only knew what God can give you, and if you only knew who it is that is asking you for a drink, you would ask him and he would give you living water."

"Pardon me, sir, but I notice that you don't have a bucket and this well is deep. How are you going to be able to give me living water? Jacob, our ancestor, who used this well for his family and flocks and who gave it to us, couldn't do that. Are you greater than he?" the woman asked.

"But I am not talking about this water," Jesus

explained patiently. "Drink of this water and you will soon get thirsty again, but drink of the water I can give you and you will never suffer from thirst again. The spiritual water that I can give you will be like an inner spring of Life always welling up inside you."

"Sure," the woman replied, "that's the kind of water I would like to get. I'd like it if I didn't have to come all the way out here to draw water." She still did not see the meaning of Jesus' talk about "living water."

So Jesus took a different tack, no more obscure language. "Go home and get your husband to come back with you."

"I don't have a husband," she said quickly.

"I know you don't," Jesus returned. "And you answered truthfully, because you have had five husbands and the man with whom you are living now is not your husband."

"Wow!" she thought out loud, "this stranger couldn't know that unless he were a prophet of God. Now I'll ask him something I've always wanted to know. . . if I ask God to forgive me, where should I do it? Where is the right place to worship, anyway?"

"Sir, our ancestors worshipped here on Mount Gerizim; you Jews say that the right place to worship God is in the temple of Jerusalem. Which is right?"

"Believe me," Jesus replied, "the time is soon coming when neither place will be necessary for the true worship of God. Right now the answer would have to be that the Jews are more correct in our worship of God because you Samaritans have been misled in the past, but it is time now for the real worshippers of God to worship in spirit and in truth. That is what God really wants since God is Spirit, not bound to any physical place."

By now the truth that is dawning on the woman in Samaria should be obvious to everyone who shares the religious tradition common to both Jews and Samaritans. She says, "I know that someday the Messiah is coming. And He will make everything plain to us." And Jesus is fully revealed:

"I, who am speaking to you right now, am the Messiah. Your waiting is over."

The disciples who had gone into town interrupted the conversation. Astonished to find Jesus talking with a woman, a thing no religious teacher would do in public, they couldn't even bring themselves to ask "What are You doing? Why are You talking with this woman?"

It was then that the woman broke for home, so excited about what Jesus had just said that she forgot the water bucket she had come to fill. Every person she met as she ran into town caught her excitement.

"Come out to the well and I'll show you a prophet who told me everything I ever did. Couldn't this be the Messiah?"

When she came back she was no longer alone; a big crowd of curious towns folk came with her.

Meanwhile, the disciples showed Jesus the food they had bought in town.

"You had better have something to eat," they urged Him.

His reply to them about food was the same kind of remark He had made earlier to the woman about water:

"I have food to eat that you don't know about!"

"What's this?" they said to one another. "Has somebody else brought Him something to eat while we were gone?"

"No," Jesus assured them, "I mean that it is meat and drink for me to do the will of God Who sent me until I have finished that work. You know the old proverb: 'If you sow the seed you must wait for four months until the harvest can come.' But," possibly gesturing toward the crowd of people coming out from town, "look around you at these fields for our work. They are ready to be harvested now. There is no waiting; the harvester and the planter can celebrate together as the prophets dreamed.

"Remember, too, another old saying: 'One sows and another reaps.' Already I have sent you out to reap a crop which you neither sowed nor cultivated. Your harvest is the result of the labor of other people."

And the harvesting began; many of the people of Sychar believed in Jesus because of the personal witness of the woman who kept telling them, "It's unbelievable; He told me everything I ever did!" They persuaded Jesus to extend His lunch stop to two days with them and, as a result of hearing Him themselves, many more of them put their faith in Him.

"At first we listened to Him because of what you told us," they said to the woman, "but now we have met Him ourselves, and we know that He is indeed the Savior of the world." (4:1-42)

The Gospel writer wants all his readers to have that same experience. Now, after the two days, He headed north again, back home to Galilee, even though He Himself had said that the only place a prophet is not honored highly is in his own country. However, many Galileans welcomed Him because a lot of them had been in Jerusalem for the Passover days and had seen and heard what Jesus did there. Bypassing Nazareth, He went again to Cana, the town where the water had been turned into wine.

In Capernaum there was a government official whose son was sick, and when he heard that Jesus was back in Galilee he hurried over the twenty miles to Cana to beg Him to come down to Capernaum and heal the boy.

"Unless you see signs and a miracle performed you won't believe," Jesus said, watching to catch the man's reaction. Faith has to go deeper than sight.

Not daunted, the official who had humbled himself to come to Jesus replied immediately, "Sir, I know that You can heal my son; please come down with me."

"With such faith you can go back by yourself," Jesus said; "your son will be all right!"

While he was on his way back, some of his servants met the man from Capernaum and told him that the boy was healed.

"Exactly when was it that the boy began to recover?" he asked them.

"At one o'clock yesterday afternoon the fever left him," they answered. And the father knew for certain what he had already guessed, that it happened exactly when Jesus said to him "Your son will live!"

This was just one more sign of His Messiahship by which people who didn't even know Him came to believe that He had the power of God. The official and all his household said that it made believers out of them. (4:46-54)

Another miracle that highlighted Jesus' mission occurred back in Jerusalem again when Jesus had returned for another one of the three great religious feasts which all Jewish men were expected to attend.

Near the sheep gate of the walled city was a pool called Bethzatha (or Bethsaida). On five porches around it a good many invalid people, with various ailments, waited for a chance to be healed. The common superstition was that an angel would make the waters bubble up (since the pool was fed by an underground stream which did cause it to be disturbed occasionally), and the first one in when that occurred would be healed. One man had been there for thirty-eight years. When Jesus found out about this man He went over to him.

"Do you want to be healed?" Jesus asked him (a question that is not so odd when you consider that many of us would rather be treated as invalids).

"Oh yes, Sir, I try to get down the steps into the pool everytime the water begins moving, but without help I can't get there before somebody else can step into the water. I'm still trying."

"Then get up right now, pick up your pallet and walk!" Jesus commanded.

As the realization of healing swept over him, the crippled man stood up by himself, picked up his pallet as Jesus had told him to do, and began to walk!

Then, religious Law which puts rules ahead of people raised its ugly head. It was the sabbath day, and some rules-keepers actually confronted the man who was now walking on his own:

"Didn't you know that you are breaking the sabbath law? It is not lawful for you to carry your pallet on the sabbath; that is forbidden work."

"Maybe," the healed man answered, "but the man who has just healed me told me to pick up this pallet and walk, and that's what I am doing!"

"Oh yeah? Show us this man who told you to carry this pallet today. Where is he now?"

Looking around, the healed man had to say "I don't know," because Jesus had moved away through the crowd of people who were there. But later that day in the temple Jesus sought him out and said to him, "Well, look, you are healed! Now see that you are careful not to sin, or something else worse may happen to you."

Now that the man had discovered who it was that had healed him, he told everybody; and this healing on the sabbath was one more cause for the Jewish religious opposition to Jesus. But when they jumped Jesus about it, His reply was "My Father God is working still, and so I am." That was even worse: not only did Jesus break the sabbath laws, but He called God His father which gave them reason to charge Him with blasphemy, making Himself equal with God.

Jesus reasoned with them this way: "The Son only does what He sees the Father doing; what the Father does the Son does likewise. Isn't that the way it should be? The Father loves the Son and shows Him what He is doing, and He will reveal even greater things than you have already seen. The Father raises the dead to give them new life; the Son will too. The Father allows the Son to act so that everyone will honor the Son as they do the Father. So those who do not honor the Son really do not honor the Father.

"I will make it plainer: the person who hears my word and believes the One Who sent me has eternal life. That person needs no final judgment because he/she has already passed from death to life. We have now come to the hour when the spiritually dead will hear the Son of God and will live if they heed. The very life of the Father is also in the Son, and the Messiah has been given by God the authority to make judgment, a judgment that will extend even to those who are now dead and buried. He will call forth the good to be resurrected to new life, and the evil will be raised to face their judgment.

"You see, I actually cannot do anything on my own authority. The judgments I hear God making I pass on to you, and my judgment is just because I only try to express God's will, not my own.

"If I were my only witness, naturally you may not believe me; but I have another witness who backs up my word. Even greater than John, whom you held in such high regard, is this witness. You can see this approval of my word and work in the fact that God allows me to accomplish these things. The work I am doing is its own witness that the Father has sent me. God has no physical presence and you have never heard God's voice, nor do you know the inner Presence of God. If you did, you would believe the

One God has sent.

"You are always busy searching the scriptures because you think that somehow in them you will find the key to Eternal Life. Well, it is those very scriptures that bear their witness to me, and still you refuse to believe me so that you could have that Life for which you are searching.

"It isn't praise from people that I am looking for, but I can see that you don't have the love of God in you because you don't believe me when I come only in God's name. If someone came on his own claiming to be the Messiah, you would follow him. But then how could you believe me? You are always looking for praise and confirmation from one another instead of seeking only confirmation from God. It is not just I who accuse you, but Moses' own words do too. If you believe the words of Moses you would believe me because Moses wrote about me, but if you won't believe his writings which you hold to be the key to life, then naturally you won't listen to me. (5:1-47)

FURTHER REVELATION. . .
of Who Jesus was came to those who were with Him during a time when He was on the east side of the Sea of Galilee, which may be known to you as the Sea of Tiberias. He had crossed the narrow sea by boat, and a big crowd followed around the end of the lake because they had seen the healing miracles He performed. Jesus was sitting on a hillside with a few disciples when the crowd caught up to them. In addition to those who had followed around the lakeside, the crowd was made even larger by pilgrims passing by on the way to Jerusalem for the Passover celebration.

Seeing the crowd coming, Jesus turned to Philip who was from nearby Bethsaida and asked, "Where are we going to find food enough to feed all these people?'' We know that Jesus was only testing Philip to see how he would react, because Jesus already knew what He was going to do.

''It would take more money than we have to get enough bread just to give each one a little piece,'' Philip observed.

''Yes, but there is a little boy here who has five barley loaves and two fish,'' Andrew offered. Then he added realistically, ''But what is that among so many people?''

Jesus took command now. ''Tell the people to sit down on the grass,'' He told the disciples. There were about five thousand of them who watched as Jesus took the five little loaves, said a prayer of thanks to God and then began to distribute the bread to those who sat nearest Him. He followed the same procedure with the two small fish, and the wonder of it all was that there was more than enough bread and fish to go around. In fact, everybody had all they could eat.

Finally, Jesus told His disciples ''Don't waste anything. Gather up everything that is left.'' It took twelve baskets to carry it all. That did it; ''There is no doubt that this is the prophet Moses predicted!'' Excitement ran so high among them that Jesus could see that they would try to force Him to lead their rebellion against Rome. (We always seem to want to use the power of God for our own ends.) So He slipped away from them into the hills. (6:1-15)

Later that evening the disciples got into their boat and started to make the four-mile crossing to Capernaum. Though it was already dark, Jesus had not come back down hill to join them. It was truly a dark and stormy night with a strong wind blowing against them. They were out working hard at their oars when they saw a sight that stunned them. Jesus was walking toward them on the water! He said the same thing that God's angel messengers always seem to call out to startled human beings suddenly made aware of the divine Presence: "Don't be afraid; it is I!"

Now they rallied to help Him into the boat as the storm subsided, and in no time at all they were pulling into shore.

The fact that only one boat had left, and that Jesus had not been on board with His disciples, had not escaped the attention of the people who were still at the site of the miracle feast. But since they couldn't find Jesus anywhere, the people who had come over from Capernaum got into the boats from Tiberias which had taken shelter from the storm of the night before and crossed the lake back to their hometown.

Were they surprised when they got to Capernaum and found Jesus already there!

"How. . .when did You get back here?"

"You know," Jesus said to them, "you look for me not because you see the meaning of my work, but because you got a free meal. You ought not to give so much effort to getting the food which perishes, but work for the food that will fill you for real life forever. God has enabled me to give you that spiritual food as well."

"Just tell us what works we have to do in order to win the favor of God," they were eager to know.

"Nothing! God has already done the work. Now you must simply believe and accept the One God has sent." That was Jesus' answer. We are not talking about 'works' but about a new relationship with God, John's Gospel was stressing.

The Jewish love for argument and "proofs" now came to the surface again. So some of them said to Him Who had just claimed outright to be the Messiah of God, "Show us some more signs so we can be sure. Can you continue to give us bread to eat the way God gave our ancestors the manna in the wilderness every day?"

"It wasn't Moses who gave them the bread from heaven, was it? No, it was God Who gives the true bread from heaven that gives Life to the world," Jesus answered.

"That's the bread we want," they agreed. "Give us that bread, Lord."

Then Jesus told them, "I am the bread of life. Whoever believes me and accepts me will never hunger or thirst after the real essence of life again. It's too bad that you have seen me and still do not believe, because I would refuse no one that God sends to me. I haven't come from heaven to do my own will but to do the will of God Who sent me. And it is certainly not God's will that I should lose anyone who trusts in me, but should give that one life here and life beyond the resurrection. God wants everyone who joins me to have eternal life."

Offended religious people sharply criticized Jesus for saying that He was "the bread that came down from heaven:"

"We know his father, Joseph, and his mother. How does He get away with saying that He came down from heaven?"

Jesus simply answered, "There is no use complaining among yourselves about my human origin. The fact now is that no one will be attracted to me unless God draws him or her. That one will be with me to be raised up on the Last Day. The old prophets all agreed that it will be God Who teaches a person how to recognize God. They will recognize me as the one who reveals the Father God. That's why I tell you that anyone who trusts in me has eternal life. I repeat: I am the bread of life, not the kind your ancestors ate in the wilderness and then died, but the kind of bread for life that is the spirit of heaven which gives life forever to the one who makes it his/her sustenance. The bread which I give for the life of the world is my flesh!"

His hearers had to discuss that too, the Gospel writer reports. By asking the question, "How can this man give us his flesh to eat?" *John* can put the new Christian theology into the words of Jesus. "As real as eating my flesh and drinking my blood, my life must literally be taken into you. Without this God-life in you, you have no life; take this life into your life and you will have life that is resurrected to continue forever. The same life of God that I feed upon will be yours when you feed your spirit on mine. This life-spirit is the real bread from heaven which feeds your souls, not the kind of bread our ancestors ate in the wilderness to sustain physical life only."

That is the gist of what He taught in the synagogue in Capernaum, and even some of His own disciples found this statement about Himself hard to accept completely. Jesus sensed their uneasiness.

"Are you finding this idea hard to swallow? You won't find it difficult to accept the idea that the Son of Man came down from heaven when you see the Son of Man going up to heaven. It is the spirit that gives life, not the physical food we eat, and the words I have shared with you are real spirit and life. But some of you don't believe that. That is why I said that no one can commit his or her life to me unless God draws that person." Jesus knew who they were that didn't wholly believe Him, including the one who would actually betray Him one day. And, feeling uncomfortable now, a good many of the more casual followers left Him that day.

"How about you?" Jesus asked the inner circle of twelve, "will you leave me too?"

It was Simon Peter who finally spoke up: "Lord, to whom else are we going to go? You have the words of eternal life. We believe that, and we have come to know for sure that You are the Holy One of God.''

But that high note of triumph has a note of impending tragedy tacked on to it as Jesus comments, ''Yes, I know. I chose each of you; but one of you is a betrayer.'' Perhaps only Judas Iscariot knew whom He meant. (6:16-71)

Still Jesus confined His activities to Galilee because He knew the Jewish authorities in Judea meant to kill Him. Another one of the great celebrations, the Feast of Tabernacles, was drawing near and his own brothers tried to talk Him into going down to Jerusalem again.

''Let your followers in Judea see what all you are doing. Don't keep your works secret up here in Galilee. Show yourself to the wider world!'' It seemed that even His own brothers didn't accept Him as Messiah.

''No,'' Jesus said to them, ''it is not the right time for me to make my move. Of course, your time is always here so why don't you go on to the feast yourselves. People don't hate you, but those in power hate me because I am saying that their works are evil. When my time comes around, I'll be there.''

So they left for Jerusalem without Him. A few days later, Jesus did go up to Jerusalem, timing His arrival to the middle of the eight-day celebration. The Jewish leaders had been looking for Him, and people everywhere in the city were talking about Jesus.

''He is a good one,'' some of them would say. But others would give their opinion that He was a popular preacher who was leading people astray from the old traditions. Most of the conversations were kept private because they knew the authorities were out to get Jesus and they were afraid to be linked with His movement. But right in the middle of feast days, Jesus Himself showed up in the temple and began to preach.

''This man has never had any formal education.

Where did He get such learning?'' some of the Jewish leaders asked themselves.

Jesus answered them Himself. ''My teaching is not mine; it is God's. And if anyone really wants to do the will of God he will know whether this teaching is from God or that I am speaking merely on my own authority. The speaker who has no authority but himself is merely trying to get glory for himself, but the one who is concerned only for the glory of the one who sent him is a true messenger, and there isn't anything fake about him.

''Moses gave you the Law, but none of you keeps it all. Why do you try to kill me when you say I break the law?''

''You must be crazy! Who's trying to kill you? You're paranoid,'' some of the people said sharply.

''I do one deed,'' Jesus responded, ''and you all marvel at it (the healing of a person on the sabbath). Moses commanded the rite of circumcision for male infants on the eighth day and you do the work of performing the medical act of circumcision even on the sabbath. So, in order to keep the law you will cut a man on the sabbath but you get angry with me when I make a man's whole body well on the sabbath! Come on now, think about it and judge fairly instead of making snap judgment just on the way things appear.''

The authorities couldn't handle Him in debate, and some of the people began to say ''If this is the man they want to kill, why do they let Him speak openly without contradicting Him? Can it be that the religious leaders really know He is the Messiah?'' Others said ''But we know where this man comes from. When the Messiah appears no one will know where He comes from!''

''Well, yes,'' Jesus answered that thrust, ''you know where I come from, but it is not where I come from that is important; it is Who I come from. The One Who sent me is God Whom you do not know, but I know God because God sent me!''

That was the last straw. Breaking sabbath and other religious laws and customs was nothing compared to Jesus' public claim to be the Messiah. The authorities were furious, but they couldn't touch Jesus because so many of the people believed Him. Their reasoning was simple: ''When the Messiah appears, will He do any more miraculous things than this man has already done?''

With the undercurrent of popular approval running strong, the highest Jewish authorities sent officers to arrest Jesus. Knowing that His time was growing short, Jesus told people ''I will only be with you a little while longer, then I will go to the One Who sent me. You will look for me then but you won't be able to find me.''

''Where does He plan to go?'' they asked among themselves. ''Maybe He intends to leave the country and preach among the dispersed Jews across the Greek world. . .what does He mean that we won't be able to come where He is?''

On the last and most important day of the great harvest festival, as the throngs at the temple joined the priests in praising God for the gift of water, Jesus' voice rang out: ''If any one thirsts, let him come to ME and drink! As the scripture says 'Living water shall flow out of that person's heart.''' (*John* adds that Jesus was referring to the Spirit which would fill those who submitted to Him, explaining that the full revelation of the Holy Spirit had not come, of course, until after the death and resurrection of Jesus.)

He sounded like one of the old prophets, and some of the people said ''This really is the prophet Moses predicted.'' Others agreed, ''This is the Messiah we are looking for.'' But as soon as religious terms are used, religious arguments are set up.

"Doesn't the scripture say that the Messiah will be a descendant of David, and will come from David's town, Bethlehem?" somebody asked in a successful attempt to muddy the waters. And the division grew in the crowd. Some of them wanted Jesus arrested, but the officers had to go back to the chief Pharisees without Him.

"Why didn't you arrest Him?" they were asked, and the answer from the security men surprised the rulers: "Nobody ever talked like this man!"

"Oh, so He is leading you astray too, is He? Have any of the religious authorities believed in Him? No! Only some of this cursed crowd of common people who don't even know the law.'"

But one of the Pharisees, Nicodemus, who had gone to talk with Jesus one night, spoke up. "Wait a minute. Before you go too far, let me ask you all a question. Does our law judge a man without first giving him a hearing to find out just what he says and does?"

Ignoring the question, they turned on Nicodemus. "Are you one of these Galileans too? Look through the scripture and see if you can find that any prophet is supposed to come from Galilee!"

Their minds were made up, and they did not want to be confused with the facts.

(Some ancient manuscripts include a section that would be chapter 7:53-8:11. It is hard to believe that the writer of *John* would have left it out if he had been acquainted with it.

The story says that Jesus went out to the Mount of Olives every night to spend the night, returning the next day to the temple for more teaching and more controversy. One morning as He sat in the temple courtyard talking to the crowd who gathered around Him, the Pharisees brought a woman who had been arrested for adultery. They forced her into the center of the circle around Jesus and loudly interrupted His teaching:

"Rabbi, this woman was arrested for committing adultery. She was caught in the very act! The law of Moses says that we have to stone a woman like this to death. What do you say about her?"

They were sure they had Him trapped this time. If Jesus said that the law should be carried out, His reputation for love and mercy would be shattered. But if He did not recommend that the death sentence be given He would be shown up as a religious teacher who breaks the religious law.

Everyone was uncomfortably quiet waiting to hear Jesus' answer. And that strained silence He prolonged by bending over to write with His finger in the sand and dust of the temple yard.

"Didn't you hear us? . . .We asked you a question. . . Are you going to answer or not?" And then they fell silent again as Jesus stood up, stretched to His full height, and said evenly, "If there is a man among you who has never sinned, let him throw the first stone at her!"

With those words, He sat down again, bent over, and resumed writing something on the ground. He was not looking at them when the oldest man stepped back, then turned to slip through the crowd. Nor did He look up while the other men followed the elder one by one. Finally, only the woman was left in the center of the circle with Jesus. Sitting up straight now, Jesus looked at her.

"Woman, where are your accusers? Didn't anyone condemn you?"

"No one, sir," she answered softly.

"Then I am not going to condemn you either. Go on out and make a fresh start, and don't sin again.")

MEANWHILE THE DEBATE CONTINUED. . . between Jesus and some of the Pharisees in the section of the temple where everyone had to come with their offerings. Again claiming the role of Messiah, Jesus said pointedly to these people who had been through the ceremony of lighting the great candelabra in the temple, "I am the light of the world. Anyone who follows me will have light for living and will not continue to walk in darkness."

"There you go again," the Pharisees countered, "bearing witness to yourself. Our law doesn't allow that as truth."

"Even if I do bear witness to myself, truth is truth. And my own testimony is true because I know where I come from and where I am going, but you don't know anything about my origin or destination. You are in the business of judging other people; I am not, and I know that in your law you have to have two witnesses before something is accepted as proof. Well, I have another witness to support my own true judgment. Father God Who sent me is my other witness."

"Oh, where is 'Father God' then? We'd like to hear Him."

"You wouldn't recognize Him," Jesus came back. "If you don't know me you don't know God either."

Angrier than ever, they still could not arrest Him because of the crowd. (8:12-20) Now the argument continues, with *John* having Jesus throw in more statements which the Christian Church held to be true about Him, each one more startling and upsetting to the Pharisees than the last.

"I am leaving soon, and then you may seek me but it will be too late. You will die in your sin and will not be able to go where I am going. (The person who isn't going toward God's Kingdom of Love can't be going where Jesus is.)

"What's He going to do, kill Himself? That would

send Him to the part of Hades reserved for suicides only. We can't follow Him there!'' (Laughter from their side.)

''You are tied to this world,'' Jesus continued. ''I am not. I have told you that if you do not believe that I am from God then you will die having missed the way to God's Presence.''

''Who did You say You were? Tell us again.''

''Just Who I said I was from the beginning. I am simply saying to you and to the world what I have heard from the One Who sent me.'' They didn't understand this to be a reference to God, but Jesus went on: ''After awhile, after I am raised up by you to public scorn, then you will realize that I do nothing except what God wants me to do. God is the only One I try to please.''

Some of the people had faith in Him, and to them Jesus added:

''You are really my disciples if you keep on doing what I am telling you to do. In your own experience you will know the truth, and this true perspective on life will make you free to be yourselves.''

The argument crowd heard that too and said, ''Free? We have never been in bondage to anyone because we are descendants of Abraham. What are you talking about, making us free?''

''I am talking about slavery to sin,'' Jesus answered. ''Haven't you discovered that everyone who sins is a slave to sin. That's a terrible bondage, like being a slave in a household. A child in God's house has complete freedom, and if you would accept the freedom I, as God's Son, could give you, you would be free indeed. I know now that even though you are descendants of Abraham, you do not share his willingness to play host to God's messenger. Instead you try to find a way to kill me because my words from God find no welcome in you. So here we are: I am speaking the message of my Father, and you do what your father wants you to do."

"Abraham is our father, we keep telling you," they snapped back.

"No," Jesus answered. "If Abraham were your father, you would do what Abraham did when he welcomed the messengers of God. I come telling you God's truth and you want to kill me. You are acting like your real father!"

Now the Pharisee spokesmen made an even stronger claim. "We are children of God, since Israel is His faithful bride. We are the legitimate children of God."

"Listen," Jesus said again, "if you were children of God you would love me as your brother. If you are from God as I am why can't you understand what I am saying? It's because you can't stand to hear what I am telling you. No, your father is the devil and you do what your father wants. He has been a murderer from the beginning, and doesn't know what truth is. It is his nature to lie. He is the father of lies. So when I tell you the truth, you don't believe me because you don't recognize the truth either. Everybody who is of God recognizes the words of God. You don't because you are not God's children in spite of your traditional assurance that you are."

"Aha, you are the one with a demon; you are the child of the devil." (The Aramaic word for "prince of devils" was very much like the word for "Samaritan," so some translations have the Jewish leaders saying to Jesus "You are a Samaritan," but it doesn't fit at all.)

"No," Jesus replied, "I am not the child of the devil, but of God, and I honor my Father while you dishonor me. That's all right, because I don't care about my own glory. God will be my judge."

Now comes an even bigger bombshell. Jesus

continues. . . "If anyone stays in line with my word, that person will never taste death!"

Shocked, they gasped out immediately, "Are you greater than our father Abraham? He died. And all the prophets died. Just who do you claim you are?"

"I can tell you this," Jesus responded, "if I am trying to glorify myself, that counts for nothing. It is God Who gives me this glory. If I were to say 'I don't know God,' I would be a liar like you, but I do know God and I keep God's word. In fact, I'll go further to say that your father Abraham was overjoyed to see this day of my appearance."

"You are not fifty years old," they tried to taunt Him, "and yet you say you have seen Abraham himself!"

"The truth is that before Abraham was, I am!"

Those final words of Jesus were the ultimate blasphemy, and the only appropriate reaction to that was, "Stone Him to death!" But while they were angrily consumed in finding stones to throw, Jesus found a way out of there. (8:12-59)

Jesus was still in Jerusalem when He and His disciples passed by a man who had been blind from birth. It gave the disciples a chance to call into question the orthodox Jewish idea that all misfortune or sickness is caused by sin. "Teacher, who sinned, this man or his parents?"

"Neither," Jesus answered. "This man's blindness is not punishment from God, but it does open an opportunity for God's healing power to be shown in him. We have to do the work of God now because we don't have forever. I am in the world now, and while I am here I am the light of the world, so I'll just heal this man now." All the while Jesus was making some clay with His spit because everyone believed that a great person's spittle was powerful medicine. Then He put the clay over the lids of the man's sightless eyes and said to him "Go and wash your eyes in the pool of Siloam."

The man went immediately, and came back seeing. The difference in his bearing and countenance was so striking that even some of the people who had known him as the blind beggar weren't sure that this was the same man. "This can't be our beggar friend; it must be another who looks like him," somebody said out loud.

"No, this is I; I am the same man," he assured them.

"Then how did your eyes get opened?" they asked in astonishment.

"That man called Jesus put some clay on my eyes and told me to go to the pool of Siloam and wash it off. I did it; suddenly I am not blind anymore. That's all I know."

"Where is Jesus now?" They looked all around the area trying to spot Him, but He was not in sight.

"I don't know," the healed man said.

The Pharisees wanted to see the man as the stories spread about his healing. Their concern was not for him but for the sabbath law which had been broken by Jesus' act. He was brought before them and the questioning began:

"We've heard that you were blind and now you can see. How did this happen?"

"A man put clay on my eyes and then I washed it off, and now I can see," the former blind man answered.

Some of the Pharisees snorted "This man is not from God; He doesn't even keep the sabbath!" Still others of them were not quite so quick to draw that conclusion.

"But how can a man who is a sinner do all these miracles?"

With the division among them, they turned their attention again to the healed man. "What do you have to say about it? You are the one whose eyes were opened."

"I say he is a prophet," the man answered without hesitation.

"How do we know for sure that this man was blind from birth, and that he was actually healed?" some of them said. "Call in his parents."

"Is this your son?" they asked the parents when they were brought in, "your son who was blind when he was born? How do you explain that he can see now?"

"Well, we know that this is our son, and we know that he was born blind, but how he came to be able to see now we don't know, nor do we know who opened his eyes. Just ask him; he is a grown man and he can speak for himself."

Even if they did know, they weren't going to say more because they had been warned that the Pharisees had already agreed to put out of the synagogue anyone who said that they thought that Jesus was the Messiah. So the council called the former blind man back into the room. They took a different tack:

"Give God the praise," they said, "not this man; we know he is a sinner."

Then, looking them straight in the eye, the beleaguered man said firmly, "You know, I don't know whether he is a sinner or not, but one thing I do know, I used to be blind and now I can see."

"What did he do to you? How did he open your eyes. . ." they began again, and the man answered in disgust, "I have already told you, and you wouldn't listen. Why do you want to hear me say it again?" Then he added, probably with a trace of a smile, "Do you want to be His disciples too?"

"You may be his disciple, but we are disciples of Moses," they fired back. "We know that God spoke to Moses, but we don't even know where this man's authority comes from."

By now, the man is gaining enough confidence to talk back to the important leaders facing him. "Isn't this wonderful?" he said. "You don't know where his power comes from, and yet he opened my eyes miraculously. You've always taught us that God doesn't listen to sinners, but God only listens to those who worship God and do His will. Nobody has ever in all human history heard about anyone opening the eyes of a person born blind. Yet this man did. How did he do that if he doesn't come from God?"

Angry now, the Pharisees gave their answer to the disciple's original question about why the man was blind: "You were born in utter sin, and now you are trying to teach us? Get him out of here!"

Jesus heard about the incident and He looked the man up.

"Do you believe in the Son of Man, the Messiah?" Jesus asked him.

"Who is he, sir. I would like to believe in him."

"You're looking at Him," Jesus said.

"Lord, I do believe. Thank You so much for what You have done for me."

"What has happened to you is a perfect example of why I came into this world, that people who are blind can learn to see. And some who think they can see may turn out to be blind!" Jesus said it loud enough for some Pharisees standing nearby to overhear.

"Are you trying to say that we are blind?" they spoke up.

"If you really were blind and ignorant, you wouldn't be held to be guilty, but since you say you see God's will, you will be held accountable." (9:1-41)

It is just a fact of life that there is one way to grow in God's plan for H.B.s and there are many ways to go in wrong directions. Here's another illustration: "There is a door to a sheepfold where the community's sheep are gathered.

"If someone won't come through the door and be recognized," Jesus said, "but tries to climb in some other way, you can mark it down that that one is a thief. The shepherd goes in by the door which the gatekeeper opens to him because he recognizes him, and the sheep recognize his voice as well. He calls them by name and leads them out of the fold to pasture; they follow him willingly, but they won't follow a stranger because they don't know his voice."

"Meaning what?" some of His hearers exclaimed.

"I'm saying that I am the door for the sheep; through me anyone can enter God's fold and find shelter and food. False shepherds who exploit the flock for their own gain are like thieves and robbers (often pictured in the Old Testament prophetic writings), but I have come that everyone may have life and have it more abundantly. I am the good shepherd who is willing to lay down his life for his sheep. Others who are acting as shepherds only because they are paid won't protect them with their lives, but will run to save themselves when danger comes like a wolf to tear the sheep apart. It is the pay not the sheep that is important to the hired shepherd. But I know my sheep and my sheep know me, and the owner-head of the household knows me because I am His own son.

"I have other sheep that are not of this fold, and there will come a day when they will hear in other nations and follow me, so there will be only one flock and one shepherd.

"I give my life willingly for all of them. Nobody forces me to give my life. I will lay down my life and I will take it up again, because God approves what I am doing and gives me that power."

Still, *John* says, His words confused Jewish listeners. Some of them were sure He was either crazy or demonic, but others kept wondering how a bad man could do the good things Jesus did. (10:1-21)

John calls it the Feast of Dedication; usually we call it Hanukkah. It celebrates each December the cleansing and rededication of the Jewish temple in 164 B.C. after it had been profaned by Antiochus Ephiphanes. Jesus was there one winter day, walking on Solomon's porch of the temple when the usual crowd of criticizers gathered around Him.

"How long will you keep us in suspense?" they asked Him. "If you are the Messiah, tell us plainly!"

"How much plainer can I get?" Jesus answered. "The works I am doing in God's Name are my witness. But you don't read that proof because you don't want to follow me. People who join me know who I am, and I know them, and they will never die because I share with them eternal life. Nobody can tear them away from me, because God is gathering this flock through me, and no one can snatch them from God's hand. God and I are one in this."

"There it is again," some of them shouted. "He's claiming to be equal with God. Stone Him as the law says!"

Jesus' only reaction was: "I have shown you a good many miracles and good works done by the power of God alone. For which one of these are you going to kill me?"

"Not for any of your actions, but for your words and attitude," they answered. "It's blasphemy when you, a human being, make yourself out to be God."

"Wait a minute," Jesus replied to that, "isn't it written in your own scripture, 'I said, you are gods?' (*Psalm* 82:6: "You are gods, sons of the Most High, all of you . . .") If the scripture which cannot be broken called these persons to whom the word of

God came 'gods,' are you going to say that the One Whom God consecrated and sent into the world is blaspheming when I said 'I am the Son of God?' No, more than the words I say are the proofs in the works I am doing. If I am not doing the work of God, then don't believe me, but if I am doing them, then believe the works even though you won't believe my words. Then you will see that I am in God and God is in me."

Again they called for officers to arrest Him, but Jesus turned and left them. This time He kept going out of town, down the steep road to the Jordan and across to the area where He first met John as he was baptizing people. As people there got acquainted with Jesus more and more, they came to agree that what John said about Jesus was true. (10:22-42)

WHILE JESUS WAS THERE...
messengers came from Bethany, the town on the Mount of Olives near Jerusalem where Jesus often visited with His dear friends Mary and Martha, and their brother Lazarus. It was Mary who once anointed Jesus with costly ointment and wiped His feet with her hair. The sisters were sending a note to Him that Lazarus was very sick.

"This illness won't end with death, but will end with the Son of Man being seen to glorify God," Jesus mused when the news came.

For two more days He stayed where He was, then told His disciples "Let's go back into Judea again."

"You know they are set to kill You there," they reminded Him.

"Every day has twelve hours," Jesus said, "and if a person uses those hours of daylight there is light enough to walk without stumbling. If he waits till the darkness comes, it is hard to make his move.

"Our friend Lazarus has fallen asleep, and I am going to wake him again."

"If he is only asleep, he will recover," they said quickly. "You don't have to go."

"I mean that Lazarus is dead already, and I'm glad for your sake that I wasn't there to save him. Now let's go to him and you will have something more to bolster your faith in me."

Now the dangerous choice was theirs. It was Thomas who voiced it:

"Let's go with Him so that we can die with Him when they take Him."

By the time Jesus and the disciples arrived, Lazarus had been dead for four days. Friends from town and from Jerusalem, two miles away, were still coming to visit Martha and Mary to console them, but when Martha heard that Jesus was coming up the road she left Mary at home and hurried out to meet Him. When they met, they exchanged greetings; then Martha said "Lord, if You had been here I know my brother wouldn't have died. And even now, it is not too late because I know that God gives You whatever You ask."

"Don't worry, Martha. Your brother will rise again." That's what others had been telling her, so she tried again:

"I know that he will rise again in the resurrection on Judgment Day, but . . ."

"I am the resurrection," Jesus said plainly. "Anyone who believes in me will live, even if he or she dies, because there is no death in my life. Do you believe this, Martha?"

"Yes, Lord, I do believe it. I believe that you are the very Son of God, the One our scriptures said would come into the world!"

Turning back to the house, she went in calmly to tell Mary "The Teacher is here now and He is asking for you."

At those words, Mary jumped up and ran to greet

Jesus Who was still standing in the road where He had talked with Martha. All the visitors in the house thought Mary was going out to the tomb again, so they followed her out of the house. But Mary was heading for Jesus, and when she got to Him she knelt at His feet saying "Lord, I just know that my brother would never have died if You had been here!"

When Jesus saw how grieved she was, and how full of real sorrow all the other people were, He was deeply moved with compassion.

"Where did you put him?" Jesus asked quietly.

"Come, we will show You."

Jesus cried.

"Look how much He loved Lazarus!" the people near Him said. And some were heard to remark "Couldn't this man who opened the eyes of a blind man have kept him from dying?"

The faith all of them had in Him spurred Jesus' resolve. He went up to the tomb, which was a cave with a large stone at the opening, and said "Have this stone removed."

Martha spoke up, "Lord, there will be a terrible smell by this time; he has been dead for four days!"

Jesus answered, "Didn't I tell you that if you would have faith, you would see the glory of God?"

At Martha's nod, men rolled the stone aside. And Jesus stood before the opening and prayed. Finally He said out loud, "Father, I thank You that You have heard me. I know You always do, but I am saying this because I want the people around me to know also that You have sent me." Then, in a loud voice, Jesus commanded "Lazarus, come out!"

No one dared breathe, and then a gasp of astonishment ran through the group as the dead man emerged from the tomb with his hands and feet tied up with bandages, and the cloth wrapped around his face and head.

"Unwrap him and let him go!"

Now many of those who had come with Mary to the tomb believed that Jesus was the Messiah sent to unwrap them all from their sins so that they could be let go in freedom to live. But, of course, the report of Jesus' latest action reached the Pharisees in Jerusalem. Immediately they called a meeting of the Council to try to decide what to do.

"This man is at it again! He keeps performing miracles. If we let Him go on, everybody will believe He is the Messiah; the Romans will come to put down a revolt and they will destroy our temple and our nation."

But one of them, Caiaphas, who was high priest that year showed the complete lack of tact for which the Saduccees were famous when he spoke up roughly, "How dumb can you get? Don't you understand that it is necessary for one man to die now instead of the whole nation, one man to die for all the people?"

Actually, Caiaphas unwittingly prophesied the truth. Jesus would die for His nation and, more than that, for all the children of God scattered around the world.

Then and there they began plotting Jesus' death, and Jesus, knowing that, did not go into Jerusalem but went into the hill country north of the city to a town called Ephraim where He and His disciples stayed for a while.

Passover was coming again, and the customary throngs were going up to Jerusalem to get ready for it. One of the chief topics of conversation among them as they stood around the temple was Jesus.

"Do you think He will be here again this year?" they kept asking each other. And all through the crowds the ears of informers were open to listen for any information they could pass on to the religious leaders who were going to arrest Him. (11:1-57)

Six days before the Passover Jesus reappeared in Bethany. Martha and Mary prepared supper for Him and His disciples. At mealtime Lazarus ate with them, but Mary came in to the dining room and did something that directed all attention to her. She opened a bottle of the costliest perfume and poured it over Jesus' feet as He reclined by the table. Then she wiped His feet with her long hair. The fragrance of the perfume (and her act of love) filled the entire house, but instead of commenting on the beauty of it, Judas Iscariot, the disciple who would later betray Jesus, spoiled the moment by saying loudly "This perfume is worth almost a year's wages. Why couldn't it be sold and the money given to the poor rather than wasted like this?" Translated, that meant "I wish I could have got my hands on that money," since Judas, as treasurer of the group, sometimes dipped into the funds for himself. He didn't have any real concern for the poor.

"Let her alone," Jesus said quickly. "Let Mary remember that she has anointed me already for the day of my burial. You have the poor with you always, but you won't always have me."

As word spread that Jesus was back in Bethany, crowds came, not just to see Jesus but also to catch a glimpse of Lazarus, now famous for having returned from the dead. In fact, the chief priests now planned to put Lazarus to death again because so many people were believing in Jesus since Lazarus' resurrection. By the next day everyone in Jerusalem heard that Jesus was coming in to the city from Bethany. A great crowd of the pilgrims went out to meet Him, waving branches of palm trees and shouting "Blessed be the One Who comes in the name of the Lord. He is the king of Israel. Hosanna!"

In keeping with the prophet Zechariah's prediction

(9:9), Jesus mounted a young donkey and rode down the winding road toward the city. (It would be later after His death and resurrection that the disciples would remember the prophecy Jesus was acting out that day.) The crowd from Bethany and the crowd who went from Jerusalem after hearing about the raising of Lazarus merged to escort Jesus through the city gate. And watching intently, the Pharisees said to one another "It is obvious that we can do nothing now. It looks like the whole world has gone after Him!" (12:1-19)

Among those who were in Jerusalem for the Passover were some Greek travelers. They had a great curiosity to see the man who was stirring up the whole city, so they found Philip, the disciple with a Greek name, and told him that they wanted to see Jesus. Philip told Andrew about the request, and Andrew went with Philip to tell Jesus that the Greeks were anxious to see Him.

"Now the hour has come for me to be glorified, but not as the conquering hero. A seed of wheat has to fall into the ground and die before it bears fruit. If it doesn't, it remains just one grain of wheat. Likewise, the person who protects his or her own life will finally lose it, but the person who is willing to give up life in this world will keep it for eternity. What is true for me will also be true for any who follow me. And any one who serves as I do will be honored by God.

"So the hour has come, and I must face it. Shall I now say to God, 'Father, save me from this hour?' No, it was for this purpose that I came to this point in time. So Father, let Your Name be honored in me." And answering from the heavens Jesus heard God's assurance that the choice of Jesus would glorify God.

The crowd around thought that it had thundered, but some of them were sure that they had heard a voice from heaven too. Jesus said, "Whatever you heard was for your sake, not for mine. Now is the time for this world's judgment; no longer will the Evil One hold sway, because when I am lifted up I will draw all the world's people to me." Those who understood Him knew that Jesus was saying that it would be a cross that lifted Him up in death.

"The scripture tells us," someone said, "that the Messiah will remain forever. Why do you say that the Son of Man must be put on a cross? You can't be talking about the special One the scriptures foretell."

What Jesus says in answer to that is certainly what the Gospel writer and the early Church could see as they recounted those last days of Jesus on earth: "The light is going to be with you just a little while longer. Better walk in it now, because when you have nothing left but darkness to walk in you won't know where you are going. Right now, while you still have the light, walk in it so that you may become children of light forever." (12:20- 36)

With that, Jesus left them knowing that Isaiah was right when he said that in spite of "the arm of the Lord being revealed" many still had blind eyes and hardened hearts. Even though He had done so many miraculous things among them, they did not believe in Him. Still, a surprising number of people, including some leading citizens, did believe in Him, but they were afraid to say so openly because they were afraid the Rabbis would kick them out of the synagogues. They were more anxious to keep the favor of other people than to have God's approval.

And Jesus went on preaching the same message: "The person who believes in me actually believes in God Who sent me. What you see in me is what God is. I am the light that shows the way through darkness. If anyone does not believe what I am saying to be true, I won't judge that person, since judging is not my purpose. I am here only to help and to save, but the truth in what I am saying will be the judge for each person on Judgment Day. Since God tells me what to think and say, you can take my words for God's, and I know that keeping God's commandments is the way to eternal life." (12:37-50)

THE NIGHT BEFORE PASSOVER . . .

Jesus knew that the end was near for His work of love. He was eating supper with His disciples when He got up and stripped off His outer garments, tucked a towel around His waist, and poured some water into a washbasin. Here was Jesus, knowing that God had put everything into His hands, knowing that He had come from God and was very soon going back to God, and knowing also that Judas Iscariot had already decided to betray Him, and He was going around the room washing His disciples' feet like a servant.

When He got to Simon Peter, Peter said to Him as if unable to believe what he was seeing, "Lord, are You actually going to wash my feet?"

"What I am doing now, you don't understand, but later on you will," Jesus answered.

"Oh no, Lord. You will never wash my feet!"

"If I don't, Peter, you won't have any part of me," Jesus replied.

Then Simon melted. "Lord, not only my feet, if that is the case, but my hands and my head too!"

"No," Jesus said to Simon and to them all "if a person has bathed, he only needs to have his feet washed when he enters the house of the host. You are clean enough, but not all of you." And the Gospel writer adds that Jesus said "You are not all clean" because He knew who was going to betray Him.

After He finished the foot washing, Jesus dressed again and took His place at the table. They were waiting for Him to speak.

"You know what I have just done?" Jesus began. "You call me Teacher and Lord, and that's right, I am. Now then, if I, your Teacher and Lord, have washed your feet, you ought to be willing to wash one another's feet. I just thought I would give you this example so that you should do for each other what I have done for you. You know that a servant is not greater than the Master, nor is the one who is sent more important than the one who sends the messenger, so if I can do it, you can too. And you will be blessed if you learn true humility in service. I realize I am not getting through to you all, and I know that the scripture has to be fulfilled, 'One who has eaten my bread has lifted his heel against me.' But I am saying all this now so that after it takes place you will know that I knew and accepted it.

"You will one day go out as my representatives, and when you do anyone who receives you kindly receives me and, of course, receives also the One Who sent me.

"And yet," He continued, "what troubles me deeply is that one of you, my cherished friends, will betray me." Instinctively the disciples looked at one another for some clue as to the one it might be. Peter asked the man next to Jesus at the table if he knew who it was, and this disciple so close to Jesus looked at Jesus and asked the question: "Lord, who is it?"

Jesus answered quietly, "It is the one to whom I give this bite of bread when I have dipped it in the dish." The disciples watched carefully as Jesus performed this act, which usually showed special friendship or admiration on the part of the host toward a guest, and heard Jesus say as He passed the morsel to Judas Iscariot, "What you are going to do, get on with it now."

Judas had the money box, so some of the disciples thought Jesus was telling him to go out and buy something for the meal, or maybe to go make a Passover offering for the poor. Without another word, Judas got up and went out, and the dark night outside was a symbol of the utter darkness that had taken over his life. (13:1-30)

Now all uncertainty is gone; Jesus knows that His arrest and death are near. His voice is as firm as His determination when He tells the remaining group "The time is here for the Son of Man to be glorified, and for God finally to be revealed completely. I will be obedient to the end and God will see that everything comes out all right. So I won't be with you much longer. As I told other people once 'I am going where you cannot come.' But before I go I want to give you this one new commandment: love one another the way I have loved you. If you stick together in this love for one another, then everyone will know that you are my disciples still."

"You are going where we can't follow?" Peter said to Jesus.

"That's right, you can't follow me now, but you will later," Jesus repeated.

"Well, I don't know why I can't follow You now," Peter commented. "I will gladly lay down my life for You."

"Is that right, Peter? I am telling you the truth when I say that the first rooster won't have crowed in the morning before you have denied me three times!" (13:31-38)

Then Jesus continued with words of assurance, "Don't be disturbed by all this. Believe in God and continue to believe in me. In God's House there are plenty of rooms; if that weren't true I would never have told you that I am going ahead to prepare a place for you. And, believe me, when I go to get a place ready for you I will come back and take you with me so that you may be where I am again. You know the way I am going."

Here Thomas interrupted. "Lord, we don't know where You are going so how can we know the way?"

"You just follow me," Jesus explained to Thomas. "I am the way, and the truth, and the life. It is still true that no one comes to God through any other way. When you know me, you know God. From now on you don't need to have any doubts about what God is like, because you have known me."

"Just show us the Father God," Philip said, "and we will be well satisfied."

"Have I been with you all this time, Philip, and you don't think you know me?" Jesus asked pointedly. "If you have seen me, you have seen God. You don't have to ask any more for God to be shown to you. Don't you really believe that God is in me and I am in God? You've seen that the words I have spoken have not been on my own authority but because God works through me. If you still can't believe that I am in God and God is in me, then think about the works you have seen and let them speak for themselves. And, speaking of my works, I tell you that people who believe in me will do similar works. In fact, you will do greater works because I am going back to Father God in spirit and I will be there to help with anything you ask in my name. Because if you love me, you will want to do what I would have you do.

"I will ask God to give you another Counselor Who can be with you forever since I can't. I am talking about God's own Spirit of Truth which most Human Beings can't receive because they don't see or know Him. But you will know Him now because the Spirit is always with you and will live in you. So I won't leave you without help; I will come to you. In just a little while, when the world can't see me any more, you will see me again. And because I live, you will be spiritually alive as well. You will know then that the circle is complete; I am in God, you are in me, and I am in you. The person who obeys my teaching because he/she loves me will be accepted by God, and will be able to see me again."

The other Judas (not Iscariot) wanted some clarification. "Lord, how will You make yourself known to us and not to other people?"

"It's like this," Jesus answered, "If a person loves me, that person will do what I say. God will love that one, and we will come in spirit to live with that person. Someone who does not love me doesn't stay in harmony with me and won't know I am here.

"I am here telling you what God tells me, but after I am gone God will send you a Counselor, the Holy Spirit, to take my place with you. And the Spirit will remind you of everything I have said plus a lot more. So I leave with you my peace, not the kind of calm of inaction that the world calls peace, but the peace that keeps your heart untroubled in the midst of trouble and unafraid in the midst of fearful times. I have said that I am going away, and that I will return. Now if you love me you will be glad that I can go to my Father God in Whom life is even more full. I'm telling you all this now, so that when it happens you will understand and keep your faith in me. We won't have much more time to talk because the forces of this world are closing in. Actually, evil has no power over me, but I go through this because God wants me to. This way the world will know that I stayed true to God to the end.

"Now it is time to leave this room." (14:1-31)

OTHER SUMMARY THOUGHTS...

Jesus left with His friends before He was taken by the authorities, *John* recalls. Chapter 15 begins with Jesus using the image of the grapevine, so dear to Israel because it had for centuries been the symbol of Israel itself.

"I am the one true vine, and my Father is the vinedresser. He has to cut off every branch that doesn't bear fruit, of course. And every branch that does bear fruit He has to prune carefully so that it will bear even more fruit. You are already good vital branches because of what you have learned from me. Stick with me, and keep my spirit in you. The branch can't bear fruit unless it stays attached to the vine; neither can you keep being fruitful unless you stay attached to me. I am the vine and you are the branches. Stay rooted in me and you will stay alive and full of fruit, but separate yourselves from me and you will not be able to do anything. In fact, a person outside of my spirit is like a dead branch of useless grapevine; it will be gathered into a pile for burning. But if you are growing in me and keep on doing as I would do, then you have all the resources for life which I have. Whatever you need God will provide, because God is glorified by the fruit you produce as my disciples. So stay rooted in my love the way I am in God's love. I am anxious that you understand this fully, because I want your real joy in life to be as full as mine.

"I told you before that I want you to love one another just as I have loved you. No one can show any greater love than by giving his life for his friends. That's what I am doing. You are my friends. You follow my orders but you are not servants; servants don't know what the Master is doing. You, on the other hand, are my friends because I have let you in on everything I have heard from God. You didn't choose me, but I chose you because I knew that you could go and bear fruit that would last. So, friends, whatever you ask now in my spirit God may give to you. Just don't fail to love one another.

"What if people hate you? You know that they

hated me before they hated you. If you were just like everybody else you would be well received, of course, but because I chose you to be different as I am different, much of the world will hate you. Just remember that a servant is not greater than the master. If they persecute me, people will persecute you; if they accepted my teaching they will accept yours also. They will do bad things to you on account of your relationship with me because they don't know God Who sent me. If I had not come to show them the right way to live, they would not have known where they were missing the mark (great New Testament definition of 'sin.') But now people have no excuse, and they get angry about that. Rejecting me they are rejecting God as well, but it was written long ago in the scripture, 'They hated me without cause.' But it is enough for me to know that the Holy Spirit of truth, Whom I will send to you, will stand up for me; and you also will be my witnesses because you have been with me from the beginning. (15:1-27)

"I have to warn you of all this to keep you from giving up and quitting someday. Your fellow Jews will kick you out of their synagogues, and it one day will get so bad that people who kill you will think they are doing God a service. They will do that because they don't know God, nor me. Just remember when that time comes that I told you it would be this way. I didn't say all this to you when you first joined me because I was going to be with you for a while. But now I am going to have to leave you, and I can see that your hearts are full of sorrow even if you don't want to talk about what is going to happen to me. Even so, it really is better for you now that I leave you, because the Counselor Whom I shall send to you can be with you everywhere.

"You can depend on God's Spirit to convince people that they sin if they do not believe in me, that my way is the right way to live because God accepts me, and that judgment is coming on everything in the world that is out of line with my life.

"I have so much more to say to you, but it would be too much for you to take now. You will learn more and more when the Spirit of Truth is with you. The Spirit will lead you into the future, informing you of God's will for you just as I have done here. More and more you will be led to see the meaning of my life and way. Every truth that is God's will be opened to you; the Spirit will help you understand it all.

"So I will leave you shortly, but then in a little while you will see me again."

"What does He mean by 'a little while'? they asked one another.

"I'll tell you," Jesus said, "what I mean when I say I am leaving you in a little while, and then a little while later you will see me again. Your sorrow at having me leave, while everybody else is glad I am gone, will turn into joy soon like a woman who forgets all the labor pains in the joy of having the baby after it arrives, so you will have sorrow now but when I see you again you will be full of joy which nobody can ever take from you again. You won't need to ask any more questions then; God will answer your every need. Whatever you need for complete joy will be given you.

"I know I have been saying things to you that you had to think through to get the full meaning, but the time has come when I can tell you plainly that I came from God and am going back to God. Because you believe that, and because you love me, God will deal directly with you. You don't need to have me ask something for you. As long as you ask in my spirit God will do it."

"Yes, that we can understand plainly," they said. "We believe You came from God."

''Now you do,'' Jesus added. ''But the hour is soon coming when you will all scatter and head for your homes, leaving me alone. God will be with me, so I won't be alone. I am telling you this so that when it happens you will realize that I knew it would, and you won't be completely devastated with guilt. You will have your share of tribulation in this world, but remember that I have overcome the world and you will yet have reason to rejoice.'' (16:1-33)

Now Jesus lifted His eyes to heaven and prayed ''Father, the hour has come, let me face it with glory so that I bring glory to You. You gave me the power to give the quality of eternal life to everyone You brought to me. Now they know You as the only true God, and they know me as the Messiah You sent because I did the work You set out for me to do. Now take me back to the glory I shared with You before the world was created.

''I have shown Your nature to the people You gave me to lead; they have learned to keep Your word. They know now that everything I had to give comes from You, and that You sent me. For these friends I am praying right now. I am not praying in general for everybody in the world now; I am asking Your help for these who belong to You and to me, and through whom my work will be completed. I won't be in the world any more, but they will be. Keep them in the spirit You gave me so they will always be as one, even as we are. While I could be with them, I guarded them and kept them together in Your Name, and none of them was lost except the one traitor who is fulfilling the scripture.

''Now that I am coming to You, fill them with the kind of joy I have had. The world is going to hate them because I have given them Your Word so that they are not based in the human world, even as I am not. I am not praying that You should take them out of the world, but I am asking You to keep them from the Evil One since they are set apart from the world for a separate calling as I am. Equip them with the truth of Your Word because I am sending them into the world as You sent me. It was for their sakes I consecrate myself, let them also be consecrated to truth.

"There will be others who will believe in me because of their word. I pray that they, too, may be made one in us and so be true witnesses to the rest of the world. Above all else, let them, because of their oneness in love with each other and with me, be with me one day to see the glory Your love planned for me before the foundation of the world. I have made Your true nature known to them, and I will continue to do so, so that the same love You have for me may be in them. Amen."

His prayer finished, Jesus went down across the Kidron valley and with His disciples entered a garden near the base of the Mount of Olives. Judas knew He would be there because it was a favorite stopping place for Jesus. So Judas led a band of soldiers and security guards who worked for the High Priests and chief Pharisees out to the garden that night. They came in with their torches and lanterns and weapons. Jesus, seeing them come, waited because He knew what was going to happen. When they got to the garden, He stepped forward into their circle of light and said, "Who are you looking for?"

"Jesus of Nazareth," several answered Him at once. Judas was right there with them.

"I am He," Jesus said calmly.

Face to face with Him, they drew back a few steps and some even fell to the ground. Nobody seemed to know what to do now. Again Jesus asked them,

"Who is it you want?"

And again someone said "Jesus of Nazareth."

"I told you that I am He; so if you want Me, then let these men go."

(He had assured God that He would not lose one of those given to His care.)

"Not without a fight," Peter thought, and he drew the sword he carried and hit Malchus, the High Priest's slave, with it, cutting off an ear.

"Peter!" Jesus' voice rang out. "Put up that sword. Shall I not drink the cup which God has given me?"

The show of violence gave them something to act upon, so the soldiers quickly surrounded Jesus and bound His arms. Back across the narrow valley they led Him. As they started up the steep hill to the city they stopped first at the house of Annas, the father-in-law of Caiaphas who was High Priest that year. It was Caiaphas, you will remember, who told the Council that it was better for one man to die than the whole nation.

In the darkness behind the armed mob, Peter and another disciple followed them. Since that disciple knew the High Priest he was allowed to enter the rather large room which was used as court at times. Peter was stopped at the gate to the courtyard of the house, but after the other disciple spoke to the maid who was stationed at the gate, Peter was allowed to enter the garden area.

"Aren't you one of the Man's disciples?" she asked Peter as he passed by.

"No, I am not," Peter answered.

By now the night was cool, so some of the servants had made a charcoal fire, and they were standing beside it warming themselves. Peter edged up to the fire too.

Inside, the High Priest began asking Jesus about His following and His teaching. Jesus answered "I haven't kept anything secret. All my teaching I have done in the synagogues and in the temple where everyone has been free to listen. So why ask me? Ask anybody who heard me; they know what I have said.

"Is that any way to answer the High Priest?" an officer standing next to Jesus shouted, and he struck Jesus with his hand.

Still calm, Jesus answered, "If I have told something wrong, go ahead and accuse me of it; but if I have spoken the truth, why do you hit me?"

That was enough for Annas. He had Jesus, still bound, hustled over to Caiaphas. Meanwhile, one of the servants standing near Peter as he warmed himself by the little fire said to him, "Aren't you one of Jesus' disciples?"

"No, I am not."

But one of the servants of the High Priest, a kinsman of the man whose ear Peter had cut off, took a closer look. "Didn't I see you in the garden with Him earlier tonight?"

"No, I tell you I don't know Him," Peter said for the third time.

And somewhere nearby a rooster crowed. (Or a Roman bugler played the "cockcrow," the bugle call that began the 4th watch of the night—3:00 to 6:00 a.m.)

CAIAPHAS WASTED NO TIME...
in having Jesus sent to the Roman governor's headquarters early in the morning. Because they would have been made unclean and could not eat the Passover meal if they stepped onto the Roman property, the Jewish leaders would not go into Pilate's rooms. He had to come out to see them.

"What charge are you bringing against this man?" Pilate asked.

The answer he got was vague. "If this man were not a criminal, we wouldn't hand Him over to you."

"Well, if He is a criminal, then take Him and judge

Him by your own law," Pilate shot back.

"Yes, but it is not lawful for us to put anyone to death, is it?"

Jesus knew that too, and that is why He knew His death must be a Roman execution, "lifted up" on a cross.

Pilate moved to his governing hall and called Jesus in.

"Are you the king of the Jews?" he asked Jesus.

"Are you asking me this because of what you think, or did someone else say it about me?" Jesus answered.

"Me? I'm not a Jew. Your own leaders have turned You over to me, accusing You of trying to be a king. What is this You have done?"

Jesus answered by saying "My kingship is not a political one of this world. If it were, my followers would fight to keep me from the hands of the Jewish leaders; but my kingship is not bestowed by this world."

"Oh, so You are a king?" Pilate asked.

"That's what you say," Jesus replied. "I was born. . . I came into the world to be a witness for the truth. And everyone who recognizes the truth understands what I am talking about."

"What is truth?" Pilate said, not wanting to get embroiled in a philosophical discussion with a man who obviously was no threat to be a rebel king. So Pilate went outside to meet with the Jews again.

"I don't find any crime in Him," he told them. "But there is a custom that every year at the Passover I should release one prisoner for you. You get to choose the one. Shall I let this man go since He has been called the 'king of the Jews?'"

"No. No." they yelled. "Not this man. Give us Barabbas!" So Barabbas, a noted terrorist, was released while Pilate turned Jesus over to his soldiers who scourged His back with whips until He was raw and bleeding. Then, with sadistic humor, they wove a crown of thorns and smashed it down on His head. They got a purple robe and draped it around Him. Then they would come up to Him saying "Hail, King of the Jews!" and then hit Him with their fists.

Pilate waited until the soldiers were tired of their cruel fun, then he had Jesus dragged outside where the Jews were waiting.

"Behold," Pilate swept his arm toward the opening gate, "I am bringing Him out to you, but I don't find any crime that He has committed." And there was Jesus still wearing the crown of thorns and the mock purple robe.

"Here He is. This is your man!" Pilate shouted. But the chief priests and their henchmen cried out in anger: "Crucify Him, crucify Him!"

"Take Him yourselves and crucify Him, because I don't find any crime He has done to deserve the death penalty," Pilate said when they quieted enough to hear.

"We do," a spokesman said. "We have a law by which He ought to die, because He made Himself out to be the Son of God!"

That kind of talk made Pilate uneasy. He went back inside the Praetorium with Jesus and asked Him, "Where are you from?"

Jesus made no answer at all.

"What! You won't answer me?" Pilate said harshly. "Don't you know I have the power to let you go now, or to have you crucified?"

This time Jesus answered. "You wouldn't have any power over me unless God gave it to you. The people who delivered me to you are guiltier than you are here."

Again Pilate tried to let Jesus go, but the Jews now used their verbal blackmail on the governor who had been called on the carpet at least twice before by his superiors in Rome:

"If you let this man go, Caesar will hear that you let a man go who claims to be a king who sets himself up against Caesar."

Pilate backed down under their threat. He had Jesus brought outside and he sat down on the official judgment seat placed in an area called "The Pavement." It was just now noon on the day of preparation for the Passover when Pilate said, with a sweeping gesture toward Jesus, "Here is your king!" To which a chorus of strident voices answered:

"Crucify Him! Away with Him! Crucify Him!"

"Shall I crucify your king?" Pilate asked with feigned disbelief.

"We have no king but Caesar," the chief priests shouted back.

And Pilate ordered the soldiers to take Jesus to be crucified. They forced Him to carry the crossbeam for His own cross up to a hilltop just outside the city wall. It is called Golgotha, "the place of a skull." There, with two other men, one on each side of Him, they hung Jesus on a cross.

Since it was Roman custom to have a placard made to carry before the condemned man, and then to be fixed to the top of his cross, announcing the crime for which he was convicted, Pilate had the sign for Jesus to read "The King of the Jews." To be sure and irritate the Jewish leaders, he had it printed in Hebrew, in Latin, and in Greek. The chief priests remonstrated with Pilate, "Change that sign. Don't say 'The King of the Jews,' but put 'This man claimed to be King of the Jews.'"

Having given in on the matter of allowing Jesus to be crucified, the governor's stubborn streak now showed itself on this small issue. "What I have written, I have written," Pilate said with finality.

The grisly business went on. After hanging Jesus

on His cross, the four soldiers charged with the execution took His clothes and divided them among themselves by shooting dice. However, His tunic was all one woven piece and they didn't want to cut it apart, so they gambled for it and so fulfilled the words of *Psalm* 22:18: "They parted my garments among them, and for my clothing they cast lots."

As the soldiers did their work, Jesus' mother, her sister (Salome, mother of James and John), Mary, the wife of Clopas, and Mary Magdalene were standing nearby. When Jesus noticed His mother and His trusted disciple and cousin, John, standing there together, He said to His mother "Woman, be his mother." And to John "Take her for your mother." And from that time on John's home was home for Mary too.

Now the terrible racking thirst of fever was a sign that life was about finished and Jesus gasped the words "I thirst." Someone took a sponge, filled it with vinegar and stuck it on a reed of hyssop (the reed used to mark the blood over the doors of the Hebrews in Egypt on the eve of the first Passover), and offered it to the crucified Jesus who now becomes the Passover Lamb sacrificed for the whole world. After sucking the vinegar Jesus said "It is finished!" and He bowed His head and died.

By no means should the bodies be left on their crosses on the Passover sabbath which would begin at 6 o'clock p.m. So the meticulous Jewish religious leaders asked Pilate to have the soldiers break their legs so the men would die faster. He gave the order and the soldiers proceeded to smash the legs of the other two men with a large hammer, but when they turned to Jesus they saw that He was already dead, so they didn't break His legs. But, just to make sure, one of the soldiers stuck a spear into His side, and stepped back as blood and water gushed out of the wound. Two more statements of scripture were now fulfilled as well: "Not a bone of Him shall be broken," and "they shall look on Him Whom they have pierced."

Now Joseph of Arimathea, who was secretly a disciple of Jesus, got to Pilate and asked for permission to take away the body of Jesus for burial. Pilate gave him permission. Accompanied by Nicodemus, the Pharisee who had come to Jesus at night one time, Joseph took Jesus' body off the cross. Nicodemus had brought about a hundred pounds of burial spices, myrrh and aloes. They wrapped the body with the spices in linen cloths in the normal way of preparing for burial.

Near the place where Jesus was crucified was a garden where there was a new tomb never used before, and since it was close at hand and they were racing to beat the 6 o'clock deadline they laid Jesus' body there. (19:1-42) Friday night, Saturday (the sabbath), and Saturday night, the friends of Jesus waited to be able to complete the burial.

EARLY SUNDAY MORNING, . . .

before dawn, Mary Magdalene was already out by the tomb. When she got there she could see that the large stone had been rolled away from the entrance. Fearing something was wrong she ran back to the place where Peter and John were staying.

"Come quick!" she said, "They have taken the Lord out of the tomb and we don't know where they have put Him."

Both of them left immediately, running toward the tomb. John outran Peter and got there first. He stooped to look inside the burial cave and saw the linen cloths lying there where the body had been, but he didn't go in. Peter never hesitated. When he ran up he went on into the tomb to take a look. He saw the linen cloths there, and noted that the wrapping for the head lay a little separate from the body cloths.

Now John also came in and saw how the grave clothes lay undisturbed as if the body had simply dematerialized and left them. They weren't thinking of the scriptures that said the Messiah must rise from the dead, but they believed Jesus had on the basis of what they had seen with their own eyes. So they went back to their rooms to think about it. Mary stayed outside the tomb still crying, but she couldn't resist looking inside the tomb again. To her surprise she saw two angels in white sitting where the body of Jesus had lain, one near where the head had been, the other at the feet position.

The angels spoke. "Woman, why are you crying?" (It didn't seem unnatural to Mary to be talking to angels about Jesus.)

"Because somebody has taken away the body of my Lord, and I don't know where they have taken Him." With that, Mary turned around to see who was now standing behind her. She didn't know that it was Jesus Himself. Jesus asked the same question the angels asked, "Woman, why are you crying? Who are you looking for?"

Perhaps the gardener would have some information, and, thinking she was talking with the gardener, she said "Mister, if you took Him away, tell me where you put Him and I will take care of Him."

For answer, Jesus simply said, "Mary."

Now her tear-filled eyes were wide open. "Teacher!" she exclaimed as she instinctively reached out to Him. "Yes, I'm still here; not yet have I gone back to God. So don't hold me here; hurry and tell the others that I am returning to my God and your God."

It must have hurt to wrench herself away from that spot where Jesus was, but she went back to the group of disciples in town and told them that she had seen the Lord and repeated what He had said to her.

That evening the group was all together behind locked doors since they were afraid the Jewish leaders would not be content just to put Jesus out of the way. Suddenly they were aware that someone else was standing there in the room.

"Shalom, my friends!" It was Jesus Who spoke. They could only stare in awe while He showed them His hands and His side. Then, gradually the full realization swept over them.

"It's the Lord!"

"The Father God sent me; now I send you. Don't forget. My peace be with you!" And after repeating His final commission to them, Jesus breathed on them and said "Now, receive the Holy Spirit. From now on, you will carry this forgiveness of God's Spirit to others, and will warn others that their sins are not forgiven when they refuse the Spirit."

Everybody was there except Thomas. When he came in, the others met him with the exciting news, "We have seen the Lord." But Thomas was as skeptical as they had been before they saw Jesus for themselves.

"If I could see and touch the print of the nails in His hands, and if I could feel the place where the spear wounded His side, then I would believe that," Thomas said, "but not until then."

Eight days later Thomas was with the whole group of disciples, still there in a closed room trying to decide what to do next, when Jesus came again.

Again, "Shalom!" Then He gave His attention to Thomas. "Look at these hands; put your finger here where the nails were; feel my side. I want you to believe and have faith in me."

There was no need for that. Thomas had seen all that was necessary.

"My Lord, and my God!" Thomas choked out.

"Now you believe because you have seen me alive after death! How blessed are those who will believe without ever seeing me!" Like those who read this Gospel story.

The resurrected Jesus showed Himself to be alive in a good many other ways to His disciples. Just enough is written here that you readers can honestly believe that Jesus is the Messiah, the Son of God, and in that faith you can have life in Him. (20:1-31)

However. . . if you do want one more specific story about Jesus' appearing, not as a ghost or spirit or figment of imagination but as a real person Who could reveal Himself in a complete physical body, this one is added:

Peter, Thomas, Nathanael, James and John and two other followers of Jesus were back home by the Sea of Galilee. "I'm going fishing," Peter said one day in the late afternoon. "We're going too," the others said.

As usual, they went out after dark to spend the night casting their nets from their boat, but when morning began to dawn they still had not caught anything worth keeping. Just as light began to streak the dark sky, someone standing on the shore called out to them:

"Boys, are you catching anything?"

It was Jesus, but they couldn't distinguish Who it was in the pale dawn.

"No, not here," they yelled back.

"Throw your net over on the right side of your boat; that's where they are!"

This time they threw the net where Jesus had suggested and they hit it big. The net closed around so many fish that they had a hard time dragging them to the boat. But in the midst of the excitement, John was looking at the One Who had called to them.

"I think it is the Lord!" he shouted to Peter.

"Forget the fish," Peter thought, "I'm going in to

see.'' And because no one greets another without being fully clothed, Peter scrambled to put on his cloak and jumped into the water on the shallow side of the boat to get to shore as fast as he could. The other disciples rowed the boat in quickly since they were only about a hundred yards off the beach, dragging the net full of fish after them. When they got out on land, they saw a charcoal fire there with some fish cooking over it, and some bread near the fire. Jesus spoke first,

''Bring some of the fish you just caught so we can cook some more.''

Peter was the first one to the boat so he hauled the net up. It's a wonder the net was not torn because there were 153 good-sized fish in it.

''Come on over and have breakfast,'' Jesus invited, but they were all so amazed at seeing Him that they didn't know what to say though this was the third time He had revealed Himself since His resurrection. They sat tongue-tied while Jesus served them bread and fish.

Again it was Jesus Who broke the silence:

''Simon, son of John, do you love me more than all these things?''

There is no cocksure bragging now about what he will or won't do. Peter simply replies,

''Yes, Lord, You know I Love You.''

''Then feed my lambs,'' Jesus said.

But after a few moments of silence, Jesus asked again,

''Simon, son of John, do you love me?'' And again Peter answered quietly,

''Lord, You know I love You.''

''Take care of my sheep.''

Silence. Then a third time, and perhaps Peter was remembering the three times he denied knowing Jesus, the question came:

"Simon, son of John, do you love me?"

Completely subdued under the hammer blows of Jesus' quiet questions, Peter is trying to fathom the depth of Jesus' probing. "Lord, You know everything; You know that I love You."

And again Jesus said, "Feed my sheep." Then He added, "You can believe this for the truth. When you were young, you buckled up your belt and went anywhere you wanted to go, but when you are old you will stretch out your arms and somebody else will tie you up and take you where you will not want to go." (This was Jesus' way of telling Peter how he would die for God's glory, the writer adds.)

Then Jesus' last words to Peter and the other fishermen were like His first on that same seashore:

"Follow me."

(P.S., the writer adds: As they started down the road together into the future, Peter turned and saw John behind them. "Lord, what about him?"

"If I want him to stay alive until I return again, what difference does that make to you? You follow me!" Jesus answered.

That's how the idea got spread around the churches that I may live forever, but Jesus didn't say that. He simply said that it wasn't any of Peter's business as to when or how I am to go. So I've lived long enough to bear witness to all these things I've been telling you, and you can believe they are true.

Of course, there are many other things that Jesus said and did. If someone could write them all, the world probably wouldn't be large enough to hold all the books.)

****** ****** ******

So John ends here, with the writer feeling that he has added stories that needed to be known in addition to the Gospel accounts the churches already had in their possession. And he had tried to make sure that every reader and hearer put the right interpretation on Who Jesus was and what Jesus meant:

. . .Jesus, the very essence of God the Creator,

. . .sent from life with God somewhere in glory to be a real Human Being in a real human situation,

. . .the Messiah long expected by the Jews, as the scriptures witness,

. . .Himself the witness to the truth for life that alone can save all human beings everywhere,

. . .the light of the world,

. . .the perfect illustration of what God means a Human Being to be,

. . .the eternal revealer of the heart of God which forgives, loves and reproves with only one aim; that every person in the whole world should have life and have it more abundantly.

AVAILABLE NOW!!!

HUMAN BEING & HIS/HER BIBLE ADVENTURES

VOLUME 1
"A GOD IN THE BUSH IS WORTH TWO IN THE HAND"
Genesis—Deuteronomy

VOLUME 2
"PROMISES, PROMISES"
Joshua—II Samuel

VOLUME 3
"KINGS OF THE HILL"
I Kings—Nehemiah

VOLUME 4
"THE RACE TO GRACE"
Esther—Song of Solomon

VOLUME 6
"PROPHET POTPOURRI"
Ezekiel—Malachi

VOLUME 7
"JESUS: THE WHOLE IN ONE"
Matthew—John

Now you can understand and enjoy the entire Old Testament. All six volumes of George Harper's series are available:

—Individual books — $5.95 each
—Complete Old Testament set of six — $30.00

COMING!!!

The rest of the New Testament and the Apocrypha

Available from:
H.B. PUBLICATIONS
38 Cloverview
Helena, Montana 59601

Books are $5.95 each
5 or more copies of the same title, only $5 each)